M400714484

FROM SOLDIERS

TO CITIZENS

THE SOCIAL, ECONOMIC AND POLITICAL
REINTEGRATION OF UNITA EX-COMBATANTS

**J GOMES PORTO, IMOGEN PARSONS
AND CHRIS ALDEN**

ISS MONOGRAPH SERIES • No 130, MARCH 2007

CONTENTS

ACKNOWLEDGMENTS

The research and publication of this monograph were made possible by the generous funding of the Swedish International Development Cooperation Agency (SIDA), the Swiss Federal Department of Foreign Affairs, and the Norwegian Institute of International Affairs (NUPI), through the African Security Analysis Programme at the ISS.

The project "From Soldiers to Citizens: A study of the social, economic and political reintegration of UNITA ex-combatants in post-war Angola" was developed jointly by the African Security Analysis Programme at ISS, the London School of Economics and Political Science (LSE), and the Norwegian Institute for International Affairs (NUPI). In addition, the project established a number of partnerships with Angolan non-governmental organisations (NGOs), including Development Workshop (DW), CARE Angola, and the Agency for Cooperation and Research in Development (ACORD).

The participation of our Angolan partners was an essential component of the project's development; their role throughout the project was invaluable. From active and enthusiastic collaboration in the project's design and planning, to critical research and logistical support *in situ*; from the participation in the project's interim workshop in Johannesburg to a review of findings during the project's last visit to Luanda in July 2005, this project would not have been possible without their support. The authors would like to express their gratitude to Allan Cain, Carlos Figueiredo and Moisés Festo of Development Workshop; Guilherme Santos of ACORD and Douglas Steinberg and Felisberto Ngola of CARE Angola.

The authors would like to express their sincere thanks and appreciation to the various organisations and Angolan government departments that participated in the project's interim workshop in Johannesburg during September 2004. These included Dr José António Martins of the Ministry for Assistance and Social Reintegration (MINARS), Brigadier Domingos Costa and Eduardo Martins of the Institute for the Socio-Professional Reintegration of Former Combatants (IRSEM), Lisa Maier of the World Bank, Olaf Handloegten of GTZ Angola, and General Zacarias Mundombe of the

Centre for Strategic Studies of Angola (CEEA). The authors would also like to thank Ana Leão for her very useful comments and suggestions made during earlier drafts of this monograph.

This monograph is dedicated to Mário Adauta, whose encouragement and insight formed part of our understanding of this complex country.

ABOUT THE AUTHORS

Dr João Gomes Porto is a lecturer at the Department of Peace Studies, University of Bradford. In his previous capacity as head of the African Security Analysis Programme at the Institute for Security Studies (ISS) he managed a multi-disciplinary team of researchers dedicated to the on-going analysis and provision of policy options on conflict situations in Africa. Prior to joining the ISS in 2002, Dr Porto was a sessional lecturer in Conflict Analysis and Resolution at the University of Reading's Graduate School of European and International Studies, as well as a teaching assistant at the University of Kent at Canterbury. Dr Porto holds a PhD degree in International Conflict Analysis from the University of Kent at Canterbury.

Imogen Parsons is a PhD student at the London School of Economics, in the Department of International Relations. She holds a Masters in Development Studies from the School of Oriental and African Studies (SOAS) and first class honours in Modern Languages from Cambridge University. She has previously worked in Madagascar and China for Voluntary Services Organisation (VSO) and has travelled extensively in Southern Africa.

Dr Chris Alden is a Senior Lecturer at the London School of Economics and Political Science (LSE). Dr Alden has written extensively on disarmament, demobilisation and reintegration (DDR) issues in Southern Africa, especially with respect to Mozambique, and has conducted research consultancies on the topic for GTZ, as well as having received a US Institute for Peace grant and a MacArthur Post-Doctoral Fellowship at Cambridge University. He is also the author of, amongst others, "Lessons from the Reintegration of Demobilised Soldiers in Mozambique", *Security Dialogue*, 33 (30), 2002, and "The Issue of the Military: UN demobilisation, disarmament and reintegration in Southern Africa", *International Peacekeeping*, 3 (2), 1996. Dr Alden lectured on conflict and Africa at the University of the Witwatersrand, Johannesburg, from 1990 to 2000.

LIST OF ACRONYMS

ACORD   Agency for Cooperation and Research in Development

ADRA   Agency for Rural Development and the Environment

ADRP   Angola Demobilisation and Reintegration Programme

CEEA   Centre for Strategic Studies of Angola

DD&R   Demobilisation, Disarmament and Reintegration

DW   Development Workshop

FAA   Angolan Armed Forces

FAEM   National Entrepreneur Support Fund

FAS   Social Support Fund

FDES   Economic and Social Support Fund

FMU   UNITA's Military Forces

FNLA   National Front for the Liberation of Angola

IDP   Internally Displaced Person

INEFOP National Institute for Employment and Training

IRSEM   Institute for the Socio-professional Reintegration of Former Combatants

JMC   Joint Military Commission

MDRP   Multi-country Demobilisation and Reintegration Programme

MINARS Ministry for Assistance and Social Reintegration

MPLA   Popular Movement for the Liberation of Angola

MSF   *Médicins sans Frontières* (Doctors without Borders)

OCHA   Office for the Coordination of Humanitarian Affairs (UN)

PAR   Rehabilitation Support Programme

PIP   Public Investment Programme

SSR   Security Sector Reform

UNITA   National Union for the Total Independence of Angola

INTRODUCTION

Demilitarisation in the Angolan Context

> We need to disarm in our minds first. We need agreement on what
> kind of life we want to live, what kind of society we want, what
> kind of nation we want to be. We believe that the war as such
> is an expression of the frustration and other motives that are in
> people's minds. That physical confrontation only takes place when
> the confrontation within the mind no longer has space. So it is
> important that [after] silencing the guns, we get to the stage where
> we can talk about the real issue[s] that brought conflict between
> us. Many Angolans, especially those younger ones who were born
> in the 70s and 80s, know nothing else except the war. So the only
> mentality they have is how to eliminate others to keep [themselves]
> alive and how to survive the troubles that the war brings. So, we
> have to make sure that people don't think that's the normal way of
> life, that there is a proper way of living without conflict.[1]

Demilitarisation of conflict and society is crucial to building sustainable
peace in countries emerging from the scourge of civil war. As longstanding
conflicts come to an end, a variety of approaches are adopted by national
governments and international agencies aimed at supporting processes
that facilitate this potentially volatile transition from formal peace to social
peace. At the heart of the exercise is the necessity of transforming the
culture and the instruments of war – in particular, demobilising, disarming
and reintegrating former combatants into society as well as ridding the
wider society of arms.

The experiences of controlled processes of demobilisation, disarmament and
reintegration (DD&R) in the past two decades have demonstrated that DD&R
must per force be regarded as a tool of development aid. This is particularly
true as regards programmes for the reintegration of former combatants into
society, "no longer merely seen as a humanitarian issue but...recognised
as a vital element of conflict prevention and a critical precondition of any
security sector reform".[2]

While the process of societal demilitarisation must stem from a commitment by all to an end to using violent means in the resolution of disputes (most importantly by the leadership of armed movements), if it is to lead to sustainable peace, a deeper commitment at a socio-political level amongst those individuals (perpetrators of conflict) and communities (supporters or victims of conflict) to move beyond the identities and emblems which serve to perpetuate violence is critical. Moreover, the emergence of a new social contract in post-war societies is a vital step towards re-legitimising (in many instances, creating) the institutions and culture of good governance, of which democratic elections are a critical threshold. These can serve as a litmus test of the degree of reconciliation in a post-conflict situation.

In addition, genuine demilitarisation is only possible when all constituent elements of society are able to function fully as citizens. Former combatants, while numerically small relative to other vulnerable groups such as internally displaced peoples (IDPs), are not only potentially disruptive elements in the aftermath of war, but their reintegration back into society is widely thought to present very specific challenges. In this sense, while social acceptance and economic activity form part of the basis for this reconciliation, these factors must be accompanied by some form of political participation for reintegration to be considered complete. The sublimation of the instinctive resort to arms when conflict rears its head, and its substitution with the 'cut and thrust' of non-violent dispute resolution (including, of course, parliamentary debate and judicial appeals), is the key indicator that a democratic peace has been achieved.

The twin challenges of demilitarisation and democratisation are most starkly evident in the case of Angola. No other post-conflict situation has been faced with all the complexities and challenges of failed demobilisation, disarmament and reintegration (DD&R) processes. No other protracted conflict has experimented with as wide a variety of experiences, ranging from United Nations (UN)-inspired programmes to joint foreign-national efforts, as Angola has in the past two decades. In fact, this latest attempt at a comprehensive DD&R programme represents the third Angolan attempt at a structured demilitarisation of their war-torn society.[3]

Yet, this time, the situation is fundamentally different because peace came largely through military victory. The death in combat of Jonas Savimbi, leader of the National Union for the Total Independence of Angola (UNITA) in February 2002, and the signing of a Memorandum of Understanding between the belligerents two months later, established formal peace in Angola, at last.[4] As we have pointed out elsewhere, "the Angolan Armed

Map 1: Areas Open for Humanitarian Activities, November 2002

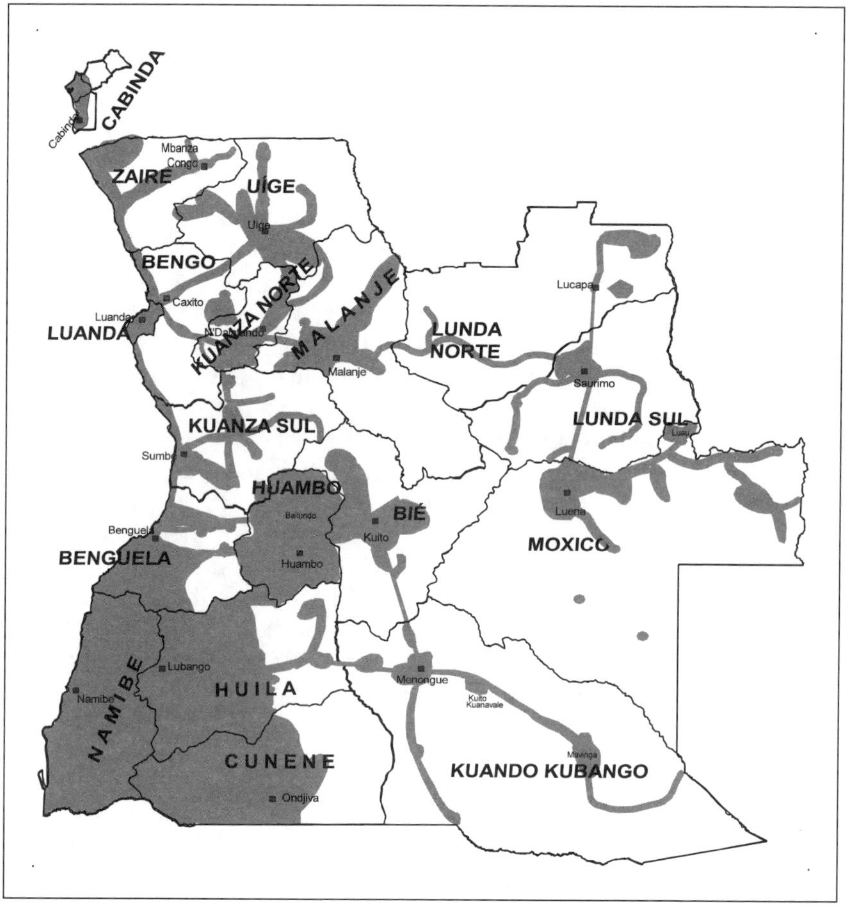

Forces' (FAA) undeniable victory over a severely weakened UNITA must be considered central to this conflict's ripeness for resolution – and this, more than any other factor, helps explain the pace at which the belligerents agreed on a comprehensive cease-fire agreement as well as their unhindered political will demonstrated in the resurrection and completion of [the military aspects] of the Lusaka peace process".[5] This was also the view of UN-system organisations present in Angola at the time:

> ...the overwhelming military superiority of the Government forces, which contrasts sharply with the 'freezing' of the military stalemate that prevailed at the time of Bicesse Accords and the Lusaka

Protocol, makes peace much more likely to endure than after those earlier attempts at conflict resolution. The country clearly has its best chance yet to build a sustainable peace and move forward to economic and social recovery.[6]

In addition to a shattered infrastructure and devastated economic fabric, the situation prevailing in Angola at the end of the civil war presented severe humanitarian challenges. In fact, by mid-2002, the number of people displaced by the war had exceeded four million. When compared to the 800,000 estimated to have been displaced at the time of the Bicesse Accords (1991) and the additional 1.3 to 2 million displaced when the war spread to major urban centres in the period 1992-1994, the tasks facing the government and humanitarian agencies in the immediate post-war period become clearer. With more than a third of its population internally displaced and several thousand refugees in neighbouring countries, limited or no access to large parts of the country (as can be seen in the map below), overcrowding in urban areas and thousands of people in temporary resettlement sites, the challenges of implementing a DD&R programme in addition to the challenges of returning and reintegration its displaced population are momentous.

At the end of the war, thousands of people emerged from previously inaccessible areas, in spontaneous movements of a magnitude impossible to predict and therefore prepare for – *Medicins Sans Frontières* referred to these as the 'grey areas' of Angola (the areas in white in the map above). The scale of the accessibility problem may also be attested by the difference, registered in November 2002, between reported IDPs (4,440,056) and confirmed IDPs (1,296,303). Of the 18 provinces, five (Luanda, Benguela, Lunda Norte, Huambo and Kwanza Sul) were the worst affected, with a combined total of 2.5 million displaced. As we pointed out in an earlier work on DD&R in Angola, this humanitarian catastrophe determined the context in which post-war DD&R was undertaken,

> ...resettlement and return issues not only provide us with a picture of what in reality 'normalisation' implies and therefore a clearer understanding of the challenges facing the government in Angola's post-war environment, but they also highlight many of the obstacles and challenges that the socio-economic reintegration of ex-combatants will inevitably produce.[8]

At the municipal and communal level for example, shattered infrastructure and weak or non-existent state structures were often all that was left after

Map 2: Population Return (April to August 2003)[9]

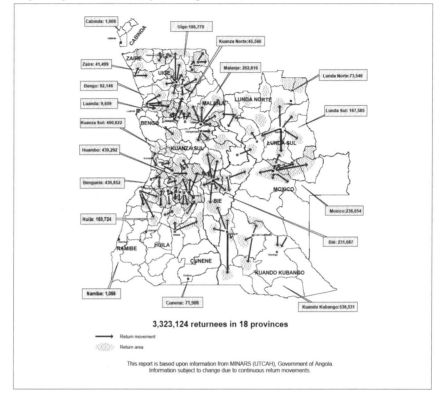

3,323,124 returnees in 18 provinces

→ Return movement
Return area

This report is based upon information from MINARS (UTCAH), Government of Angola.
Information subject to change due to continuous return movements.

the war. For the most part, the population movements described above took place without the substantive support foreseen by the 'Norms on Resettlement and Return' approved by the government during 2001. These norms defined a number of pre-conditions necessary for resettlement and return, including the establishment of security at local level, access (e.g. mine clearance), a functioning state administration, availability of land, water and basic sanitation and health facilities. The sheer magnitude of return and resettlement in the immediate post-war environment can be seen in the map below (April 2002 to August 2003).

At the same time, the first steps towards demilitarisation (cantonment, disarmament and demobilisation) of UNITA's Military Forces (FMU) began during April 2002 with the setting-up of 27 quartering areas scattered throughout the country. As mentioned earlier, the government of Angola (through the Angolan Armed Forces) retained total control of the disarmament and demobilisation process as well as the responsibility for its financing. A product of the specific circumstances of the war's ending, the government's exclusive control and financing of the process further distinguishes this process from previous attempts at DD&R in the country, as well as contemporary DD&R programmes in other African countries (for example Liberia, Burundi, DRC). No provision for formal third-party monitoring was included in the MoU, although the *Troika* (Portugal, Russia and the United States) and the United Nations were invited as observers.[10]

Two structures were created to oversee the DD&R process. A Joint Military Commission (JMC), presided over by a military representative of the government and composed of the chiefs of staff of the Angolan Armed Forces and the FMU (as well as 11 UN Military Observers), was responsible for overseeing and promoting the application of the MoU. A Technical Group (TG) was tasked with the responsibility of assisting the JMC in the performance of its duties, including the drawing-up of detailed timetables and the definition of specific activities to be carried out.

Graph 1: Evolution of the quartering process to July 2002[11]

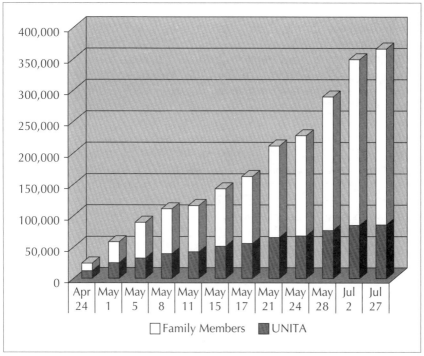

The Angolan Armed Forces (FAA) were tasked with the management of the quartering, disarmament and demobilisation of the FMU in what can only be described as a very ambitious timeframe – a mere 80 days for the completion of the quartering, disarmament and demobilisation of 50,000 UNITA combatants in 27 quartering areas. As the movement of FMU combatants towards the quartering areas intensified in the proceeding months, it became increasingly obvious that the initial time-frame would need constant revision and updating. In fact, 100 days into the process, by the end of July 2002, a staggering 85,585 ex-FMU were quartered in an expanded number of quartering areas (35). In addition, in what represented another departure from 'conventional' DD&R programmes, the government allowed former combatants' families to gather in 'family reception areas'. By the end of July 2002, 280,261 FMU family members had gathered in 'satellite' family reception areas (as can be seen in the graph below).

The commitments made in the Luena MoU, and the subsequent plans and timetables for a case-load of 50,000 former combatants, were subject to continuous revision and negotiation between the government and UNITA's Management Commission (the movement's temporary leadership structure). Internal and international pressure for the swift implementation of the DD&R programme (which would represent unquestionable evidence of an end to war and a successful demilitarisation of Angola) led to the announcement of the extinction of the FMU during August 2002 – a mere four months into the DD&R process. In a public statement, the Joint Military Commission announced that the demobilisation and disarmament components had been completed, as well as the integration of approximately 5,000 former UNITA combatants into FAA structures.

The political symbolism of the extinction of the FMU notwithstanding, the process was in fact far from complete because several thousand combatants and their family members continued to arrive at quartering and family reception areas many months later. In fact, by 18 February 2003, only five quartering areas had effectively been closed and the official figures released by the Ministry of Assistance and Social Reintegration (MINARS) at that time pointed to a total number of resettled and returned former combatants of only 22,643 and 70,694 family members.

At the time the FMU was declared extinct, demobilisation (which includes 'registration and distribution of identification documents, data collection, pre-discharge information, medical screening and transport home') was just about to begin.[12] This was confirmed by a World Bank-led mission to Angola during August 2002, which highlighted that the registration of ex-combatants and the production of demobilised ID cards were still underway while the collection of socio-economic data in 24 of 35 quartering areas had just begun.[13]

Former combatants and their families in quartering and gathering areas continued to require emergency support well into 2003. This effort, as noted elsewhere, was largely undertaken by the FAA as regards former combatants, and by the World Food Programme (WFP) and international and local NGOs as regards assistance to family members (through the distribution of food, non-food items, seeds and tools, family tracing and reunification, etc).[14] Throughout the process, the coming of the rainy season limited access to quartering and gathering areas, severely hampering resettlement efforts as well as the distribution of resettlement support kits. By April 2003, there were still 11 gathering areas and UN agencies and NGOs that reported difficulties, particularly in the highland provinces of the country, as regards the provision of basic supplies and services in the transit areas that had been created to assist the resettlement process.

By February 2003, emergency reinsertion support had been given to a total of 71,434 former combatants (equivalent to five months of salary). Yet, because of repeated delays in their resettlement and return, this money was spent in and around the quartering and transit areas, with little or no significance as regards former combatants' reintegration. For more than a year, ex-combatants continued to return to their areas of origin or chose to establish residence in new areas. Data from February 2004 points to the registration of approximately 98,252 post-Luena ex-combatants at MINARS provincial offices. Of these, 45,065 had received resettlement kits, 30,278 had received the emergency reinsertion subsidy (*subsídio de contingência*) while 5,775 had been employed in the formal and informal sectors, and 3,007 had received training through government efforts.[15]

Implementation of socio-economic reintegration programmes has, since then, proceeded at a limited pace. It has been hampered by a lack of funds and institutional capacity, the sheer scale of the problem as well as the inability of government institutions and international partners to agree on a timely reintegration programme that would closely follow resettlement and return.

While negotiations with international financial institutions for technical and monetary support, in particular the World Bank, had begun in mid-2002, it was only on 27 March 2003 that the Bank's Board of Directors approved the Angola Demobilisation and Reintegration Program (ADRP). This emergency programme (initially worth an estimated US$180 million but by September 2004 estimated at US$230 million) was designed to assist more than 100,000 ex-UNITA combatants and approximately 33,000 FAA personnel. Of the $180 million, the Bank pledged and began to disburse US$33 million (through the IDA) and US$53 million (through the MDRP's Multi-Donor Trust Fund); the government pledged US$127 million and the European Commission an additional US$17 million.

Angola also faces the challenge of reintegrating more than 100,000 former UNITA combatants (FMU) and 33,000 FAA ex-combatants (not to mention an estimated 160,000 former soldiers from two prior DD&R processes) back into society. Even though the government views the emergency phase experienced in the aftermath of the war as largely over, the considerable task of assisting the social, economic and political reintegration of these different groups remains an urgent priority. Roughly a third of Angola's population (approximately 3. 9 million people) had resettled and returned by August 2004 (including displaced civilians, refugees, demobilised soldiers and their families), while 308,758 were still displaced.[16]

Objectives and Methodology

The dynamics that drive and sustain transitions from war to peace are not well elucidated or, more crucially, studied in a systematic manner. Resources of the international community given over to the study of reintegration (in its social, economic and political dimensions) have largely focused on the instrumental concerns of policy makers – more often than not bound by tight timeframes and primarily focused on stabilisation of populations rather than a longer-term developmental and peace-building approach. The increasing realisation that demobilisation and reintegration programmes are at the core of post-conflict peace-building has resulted in the involvement of new actors in the field of demobilisation and reintegration – actors that have traditionally shied away from working closely with the military and security sectors.[17] In addition to the traditional bilateral support provided by third-party countries for DD&R and Security Sector Reform (SSR) processes, international development agencies have become increasingly important actors in these processes, in particular the United Nations Development Programme (UNDP) and the World Bank (WB) as well as a myriad of NGOs and community-based organisations (CBOs) in countries undergoing DD&R processes.

Demobilisation, disarmament and reintegration of former combatants have been given their correct place as critical components of peace-building

– a function of the risk that former combatants are perceived to pose if not adequately demobilised or reintegrated (in itself an assumption that requires further research, both context-specific and of a comparative nature), or as a result of a perceived 'peace' dividend that may ensue from the downsizing of armed forces. Yet, paradoxically, the content of substantive reintegration, from the point of the target group remains fundamentally unexamined. Key conceptual issues such as the nature of 'reintegration' and its relationship to citizenship in post-conflict societies are not properly understood or accounted for in the design and development of reintegration programmes.

This is not to say that a blueprint for DD&R processes, to be applied indiscriminately to different situations and different types of beneficiaries (e.g. regular forces, paramilitary forces, child combatants) should be aimed at. In this regard, one should note the GTZ's point that while 'good preparation and coordination can prevent mistakes and provide timely clarity about the assistance required', 'experience shows that blueprints do not exist, and that demobilisation and reintegration support is at best dealt with within the broader rehabilitation and development support'.[18] Yet, understanding the last step of a DD&R process, that of the socio-economic and political reintegration of former combatants into society – by nature a long-term process which should be linked to broader recovery efforts and development strategies – is critical. A cursory review of the available academic and policy-oriented literature reveals that, above all, the development of adequate methodologies is required so that a comprehensive and participatory assessment of reintegration processes (from the perspective of individuals and communities in post-conflict societies) can be achieved.

At a time when the reintegration of former combatants in Angola was in its infancy and several DD&R programmes were being developed in the region (Burundi and DRC in particular) the authors felt that is was critical that a project be pursued that addressed the complexities of this process with a view to critically understanding its various dimensions– not least through the development and employment of both quantitative and qualitative research methods. The project "From Soldiers to Citizens" therefore focused on former UNITA combatants in post-war Angola as a case-study, with the primary aim of obtaining a statistically informed analysis of the factors that enhance or impede the *transformation* of soldiers into civilians in a post-conflict environment.

Conducted over an 18-month period, commencing in November 2003, the project included the development of an appropriate and situation-specific survey methodology; fieldwork in three select provinces in the Central

Highlands of Angola; an interim workshop with Angolan policy-makers and project partners in Johannesburg to present initial research findings and, finally, the publishing of the project's findings.

Specifically, the project aimed to address the following questions through primary quantitative and qualitative research and analysis:

- *Which factors facilitate reintegration? And which ones impede it?* The role and type of intervention strategies that support reintegration of ex-combatants remain highly contested in both policy-circles and academia. For example, a variety of examples suggest that economic subsidies have played an important role in support of reintegration. However, as some critics have pointed out, financial support alone cannot account for what is a deeply personal experience embedded in a situation-specific environment.

- *In the absence of targeted support for reintegration, will ex-soldiers successfully reintegrate into communities? Is their experience of reintegration significantly different from internally displaced persons (IDPs)?* The imperative of providing targeted programmes to address the particular needs of ex-combatants is the rationale behind reintegration programmes. And yet, some would suggest that targeting actually inhibits reintegration back into society and that the appropriate approach would be to treat ex-combatants no differently to any other vulnerable group. Given that successful reintegration is predicated on the positive *transformation* of modalities of behaviour and, more importantly, identities formed under conditions of conflict, could special treatment aimed at ex-combatants actually inhibit or delay reintegration?

- *What then is the relationship between identity and reintegration? To what extent are self-perceptions and communities' perceptions involved in determining positive outcomes?* If the *transformation* of identities formed under conditions of conflict is a key determinant of successful reintegration, then the nature of the process has not been given sufficient attention by scholars and practitioners. Furthermore, what impact, if any, can 'extra-societal' interventions have upon this process? The importance of identity and its relationship to citizenship, the latter being seen by some as an end-point of the reintegration process, needs to be examined.

- *What does or should reintegration mean in the context of weak or non-existent state structures?* An essential feature of many (if not most) post-conflict situations in Africa – but one which seems to have been consistently neglected – is that reintegration takes place within the conditions of weak, enervated or even collapsed states. This raises the question of how one can speak of 'reintegration' back into a fragmented society, a shattered economy and often a contested political authority. Are these factors taken into account in the development of reintegration programmes?

To answer these questions, a time-series quantitative and qualitative study of reintegration in post-war Angola was conducted. Samples were used both as regards the target group (focusing solely on former UNITA combatants demobilised following the Luena Memorandum of Understanding of April 2002) as well as geographical area (focusing solely on the provinces of Huambo, Huíla and Bié in the central plateau of Angola). The choice of these three Provinces was a function of several factors, discussed at more length later on. At this point, it suffices to say that all three (but particularly Bié and Huambo) were key areas of recruitment during the war and that a significant proportion of former combatants were demobilised and resettled in the central highlands– 46,940 out of a total of 103,928 (representing roughly 45% of the total).

In-depth surveys, focus group discussions and key informant interviews were conducted to assess the levels of (i) social reintegration; (ii) economic activity; (iii) and political engagement (See Annex 1, *Survey Questionnaire*). These methods were used over a six-month period and involved one field visit to each province (two target districts, one urban and one rural in each) to collect data and information.

As was mentioned at the outset of this monograph, the project established a number of partnerships with Angolan NGOs, including Development Workshop (DW), CARE Angola and the Agency for Cooperation and Research in Development (ACORD). The participation of the Angolan partners was essential for the field research component of the project, in particular the collection of surveys, the undertaking of focus group discussions, as well as logistical support.

During November 2003, a five-day methodology test and training course was undertaken in Huambo. A core team of local researchers from DW as well as a representative from Care Bié were trained in basic research methods and the subject matter of the research. The course included activities such as small-group and one-to-one discussions, group brainstorming, role-playing and mapping. In addition, the project's methodology was tested in the field, and the feedback used in the refinement and finalisation of the questionnaire and focus group questions.

Though every effort was made to allow for the development and implementation of a survey that was both unbiased and could produce statistically sound results, the project team did experience some problems that affected the survey findings. These included:

- *Logistics*: Very poor road infrastructure, especially in rural areas, limited the time available for interaction with respondents, particularly as regards survey collection and focus group discussions. However, it should be noted that with slightly over 600 respondents, as well as focus groups and key informant interviews, these obstacles did not deter the team from developing a broad sampling base.

- *Random sampling difficulties*: There was no reliable data on the location of ex-combatants that would allow for a statistically representative sample to be generated. In both Sambo and Andulo, for example, fieldwork coincided with either food distribution by the WFP or the distribution of seeds and tools by humanitarian partners. On the one hand, this had the effect of facilitating access by the researchers to large numbers of ex-combatants but, on the other, it may have introduced some distortions into the data that should be borne in mind in later sections. Ex-combatants reporting for food handouts are already a self-selected group who are in possession of their documentation.

- *Surveying in urban areas*: In all provinces, it proved more difficult to locate ex-combatants in urban areas. It appeared that local authorities (government and traditional) were less able to identify and physically locate them within more built-up areas. In addition, ex-combatants in urban areas also proved less keen to be interviewed. What are the possible implications of this? Could it be that urban areas attract higher concentrations of ex-combatants not only because they are perceived to offer more livelihood possibilities but also because they offer a degree of anonymity?

- *Survey administration*: In some cases, local interviewers were not adequately skilled (a result of little direct experience in research techniques) making training and supervision necessary throughout the project.

- *Survey questionnaire issues*: Although the project team tested the questionnaire in the field and was able to rework the survey questionnaire in advance of formal administration, additional issues became apparent. These included questions that could have been improved by alternative phraseology and/or that would have elicited more compelling findings through alternative approaches (scaling). That being said, the overwhelming majority of questions were in fact clear to respondents and interviewers alike and did elicit substantive answers.

CHAPTER 1
ANGOLA'S CENTRAL HIGHLANDS
Provincial Characterisation and Fieldwork Review

Introduction

With an area of 1,246,700 square kilometres, Angola is divided into 18 administrative provinces with Luanda as the capital city. To the north of Cabinda province, the country borders Congo-Brazzaville; to the north and east the Democratic Republic of Congo (DRC); to the east Zambia and to the south Namibia.

Although a population census has not been undertaken since 1995 (when an estimated 11 million people were said to live in the country), the World Bank estimated Angola's population at 13.5 million in 2003. In the 1995

Map 3: Angola Political Map[19]

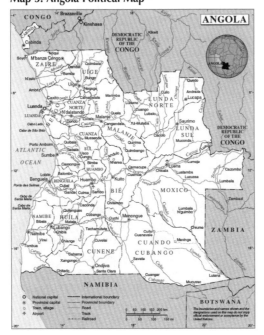

census, the breakdown of the population pointed to 49.3% men and 50.7% women, of which 32% lived in urban areas. At that time, Luanda was thought to contain approximately 3 million people.

Portuguese is the official language but several other national languages are widely spoken: Umbundo, Kimbundo, Kikongo, Chokwe, Nhanheca, Gangela and other Bantu-group languages. Angola's climate is characterised as tropical and humid in the north, subtropical with lower rainfall in the south – temperatures are usually lower and rainfall higher in the central plateau than in the coastal lowlands. The rainy season lasts from October to April and the dry season is from May to September.

Angola's political system is based on the 1991 constitution (as amended in 1992) and a constitutional review was underway at the time of this project. Provincial government is structured according to Law-decree No 17/99 of 29 October 1999 on the Administrative Reform of the State as well as Decree No 27/00 of 19 May 2000, which provides the regulatory framework for provincial governments as well as that of municipal and communal administrations.[20]

The nomination of the governor and the vice-governors remains the responsibility of the president; municipal and communal administrators are appointed by the provincial government. Provincial government relations with central government are channelled through the Ministry for Territorial Administration and, in an *ad hoc* fashion, directly with the Council of Ministers. On specific areas and issues, however, provincial governments relate on a bilateral basis with sectoral ministries.[21]

While demobilisation and reintegration occurred across 15 of Angola's 18 provinces, a significant proportion of former combatants were demobilised and resettled in the central highlands – 46,940 out of a total of 103,928 registered with IRSEM provincial offices in the three provinces (representing roughly 45% of the total).[22]

A key area of UNITA support and recruitment throughout the various cycles of war, the central provinces of Huambo and Bié (and the northeast of Huíla Province) were left with most of their infrastructure destroyed having experienced some of the fiercest fighting. The movement of former combatants to quartering areas in these two provinces increased considerably throughout the demobilisation process (as can be seen in the map above) to a total of 38,932 former combatants.

Map 4: Ex-Combatants Registered per Province – August 2004[23]

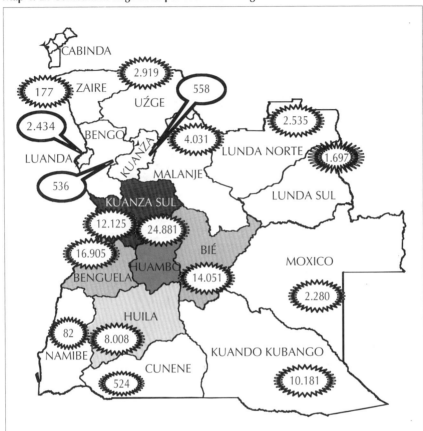

Although Huíla Province (located at the edge of the highlands plateau in the southeast) and in particular its capital Lubango, suffered less direct infrastructural damage than its neighbours, the province was affected by the arrival of thousands of IDPs. Throughout the civil war IDPs sought shelter in its urban and peri-urban areas. Lubango has retained a somewhat urban environment, making it an ideal place to study economic aspects of the reintegration of former combatants in more urbanised areas.

As will be discussed below, there are strong socio-economic similarities between these three provinces. Before the war, all three were characterised by a commercial agricultural system revolving around the production of maize, beans, coffee, vegetables and cattle farming.[24] All three suffered the catastrophic consequences of nearly three decades of civil war and unrealistic economic policies during the single-party era. Over the years, commercial agricultural production has collapsed and is now limited to subsistence farming because both urban and rural communities were forced to flee. Perhaps with the exception of Lubango, all other areas surveyed have suffered severely from the effects of the armed conflict, the social and economic fabric of their communities destroyed. A detailed description of these provinces will follow in the next chapter of this monograph.

Huambo

Overview of the Province

Huambo city, capital of Huambo province, is located at the heart of the central highlands. During the colonial period and in the immediate aftermath of decolonisation, Nova Lisboa (as Huambo was then named) was a city of considerable economic and strategic importance – in fact, and for a time, the colonisers debated whether or not to grant it the status of capital of Angola.

With an area of 32,570 square kilometres, the province represents 2.61% of the total land area of the country and is divided into 11 municipalities, 37 communes and 3,056 villages. At the time of this research, Huambo's population was estimated at 2,250,985 by the inter-agency group responsible for the on-going assessment of vulnerability to food insecurity in the province.[25] The highest concentration of people is found in and around Huambo city and in the Benguela corridor – the area of land that surrounds the (currently inactive) Benguela railway and crosses Huambo from east to west. Although the urban growth rate had been estimated at 12% and the rural growth rate at 2% in the immediate aftermath of the war[26], the province experienced an estimated 15% population growth in just nine months (from May 2003 to February 2004.[27]

The people of Huambo are primarily Ovimbundu, the largest of the three principal ethno-linguistic groups of Angola. The province, one of the most contested regions during the 27-year civil war, was a UNITA stronghold with both strategic and symbolic importance. The MPLA pushed the FNLA/UNITA out of Huambo city in 1975, and would remain in control of it until 1993 following UNITA's rejection of the results of the 1992 elections and the resumption of armed conflict – which at that time shifted from guerrilla 'hit-and-run' tactics to conventional attacks to control urban areas (later termed the 'war of the cities' phase).

While under government control the city was relatively stable, but the resumption of war in 1992 had a severe impact on Huambo's population. The city was taken by UNITA in early January 1993 after the so-called '55-day war', which saw fighting in the heart of the city itself. Although frequently bombed and attacked by government forces, UNITA managed to hold the city until 1994, when, between the initialling and official signature of the Lusaka Protocol in November 1994, the FAA pushed ahead and retook Huambo. This was widely seen as a violation of the spirit, if not the letter, of the Lusaka Protocol, causing tensions which revealed themselves as the Lusaka process began to fall apart. One of the sticking points was the administration of Huambo, with UNITA insisting on its right to govern Huambo since it had won the 1992 elections in the province and the government refusing to allow this.

From then on, the province was divided between government and UNITA control, with the lines of control moving repeatedly. Government control was concentrated around the city and the Benguela corridor, where much of the population was located. Bailundo, in the mid/north of Huambo province was Jonas Savimbi's base for most of the 1994-1998 period. Agriculture, trade and transport within the province were thus heavily disrupted and most of the *fazendas* (commercial farms) were abandoned, as will be discussed below. Once a relatively prosperous province, seen (if not entirely accurately) as the breadbasket of Angola, Huambo's population reverted to predominantly subsistence agriculture, growing maize and limited quantities of beans, fruit and vegetables.

Following the resumption of war in December 1998, Huambo again came under fire, with sporadic shelling until January 1999 and again in June of that year. As a consequence, severe levels of population displacement were noted – a movement that corresponded to approximately 17% of the province's population and followed a similar pattern to that experienced in other provinces. If unable to make their way to Luanda, Lobito or Lubango, displaced people sought safety in urban and peri-urban areas within the province (adding to the concentration of displaced people already experienced in Huambo, Caála, Londuimbale, Bailundo and Ukuma. See map below). This concentration of displacement has, over the years, contributed to serious environmental degradation: of note is the destruction of natural forests (for use as firewood) around the edges of urban areas, particularly in Huambo city during the years of war.

Map 5: Province of Huambo – Movements of IDPs 1998-2002[28]

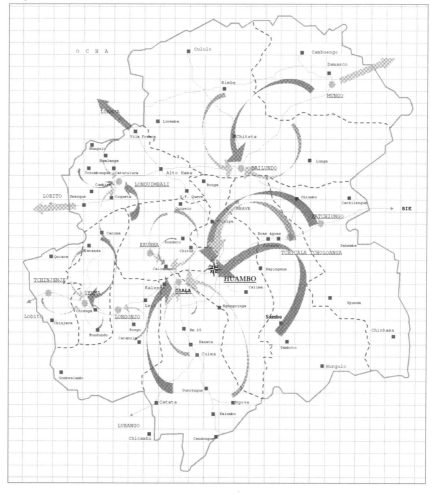

Between May 2003 and February 2004, return movements for the province totalled 14,099 people as can be seen in the table below, which details return totals by municipality:

Altitudes vary from 1,750m in Huambo's plains to 1,830m in the municipality of Chicala Cholohanga and the west of the province is a mountainous area with peaks as high as 2,620m above sea level in the *'Morro dos Moros'*. Several important rivers have their origins in this province, namely the Queve (with a basin of 23,000km²), the Cunene (with a basin of 8,600 km²),

Table 1: Population Return – Huambo Province (May 2003-February 2004)[29]

Municipality of Return	Number of people
Bailundo	10,203
Caála	117
Catchiungo	2,791
Huambo	764
Mungo	224
Total	**14,099**

the Cutato, and the Cubango. The energy-generating potential of these rivers are of vital importance for the future agricultural development of the province and they will play a critical role in the province's reconstruction.

By the time our research began, the partial rehabilitation of the road infrastructure had reconnected Huambo to other provinces in the country – yet, the majority of municipal and intra-municipal road networks remained in a very poor state. Accessibility remained significantly restricted during the period under analysis as a result of mine infestation as well as excessive rainfall which destroyed several bridges and worsened the already precarious state of much of the road infrastructure. In fact, during November 2003 and February 2004, difficult access prevented the provision of emergency food aid to approximately 204,000 people.[30]

Although the province is not particularly fertile, requiring substantial inputs in terms of fertilisers if commercial agriculture is to be developed, subsistence agriculture is widely practiced. In addition, the province reveals a strong potential for forestry and orchard cultivation (in particular avocado, passion fruit and guava), as well as for cattle farming. The total area under cultivation is approximately 502,000 hectares, with an average plot size for subsistence agriculture of 0.8 ha. Although considerably affected by the armed conflict, commercial farming has traditionally been located in Chicala Cholohanga and Ecunha.

As mentioned above, excessive and irregular rainfall during the last quarter of 2003 had destroyed much of the harvest, worsening the province's dependence on emergency support from the WFP and other NGOs, that had hoped to be able to scale down from that time. Overall, 60% of the province's maize and 75% of its bean cultivation was destroyed by the rains. Many NGOs had already scaled back their emergency presence and were focused on shifting their activities towards development priorities – in some ways a product of donor and government pressure. In fact, if anything, the level of vulnerability across the province remained considerable. At the time of the research, a significant proportion of the population continued to require humanitarian assistance (approximately 573,000 people required food assistance, of which 245,200 were considered to be in a food insecure situation). Of note is the fact that instead of stabilising or diminishing, the number of people considered food insecure actually rose by 133,000 in the five months between October 2003 and February 2004.[31]

According to official data, the province has 460 commercial establishments, 41 markets (of which 29 rural and 12 urban) and 8,900 registered traders. However, a much lower but unspecified number of establishments were effectively open for business and most commercial activity remained based in and around the provincial capital, Huambo. It should be noted that although agricultural production was severely affected in the last quarter of 2003 and first quarter of 2004, inter-provincial trade guaranteed that the prices of the typical food basket remained the same – Huíla and Kwanza Sul provinces providing the bulk of goods to Huambo. Of the 142 factories that operated in the province before 1993, only one (the Coca-Cola factory) was operating in 2003.

At the time of the research, eight professional associations and two national unions (the Angola Industrial Association – AIA, and the Grémio do Milho 'Epungo') were present in the province. Banking facilities remained inadequate; the province as a whole has three banks all based in the provincial capital. The "National Entrepreneur Support Fund" (Fundo de Apoio ao Empresariado Nacional – FAEM) and the Economic and Social Development Fund (Fundo de Desenvolvimento Económico e Social – FDES) have offices in the province but were not in operation at the time of the research. The provincial government has a number of micro-financing initiatives such as "Microform" and "Programa Novo Horizonte".

Of the 88 health units (seven hospitals, 30 health centres and 51 health posts), most had been destroyed or were in disrepair. The province has 1,246 registered hospital beds (87% are in urban areas), an average of one doctor per 111,000 people, and one nurse per 7,392 people in the rural areas. The difficult conditions and lack of infrastructure in the municipalities are largely to blame for the difficulty in attracting doctors and nurses to the rural areas.[32]

Provincial government is composed of the governor and 3 vice-governors (and their respective technical teams), as well as 12 provincial directors.[33] In terms of development programmes, the provincial government is tasked with the coordination of multi-sector programmes such as the Public Investment Programme (PIP), the Rehabilitation Support Programme (PAR) financed by the European Union, the Community Rehabilitation Programme (PRC) and the Social Support Fund (FAS). The former has been pivotal in the rehabilitation of basic social infrastructure in the urban and peri-urban areas of Huambo. In addition, several NGOs and churches have also played a critical role in implementing programmes in the areas of health and nutrition, education and training, water and sanitation, agriculture and food security, protection of human rights and de-mining. During 2003, NGOs began turning their attention to areas outside the provincial capital: 14 of these began work in Caála, 7 in Chicala Cholohanga, 6 in Bailundo, 3 in Chinjenje and 1 in Mungo.[34]

According to government data, by mid-2003 state administration had already been established in the 11 municipalities and 37 communes of the province. Yet, we should note that more often than not this was limited to the appointment of a local administrator (*administrador*) because there were other critical priorities: the rehabilitation of administrative infra-structure, the increase and strengthening of human resource capacity, and the acquisition of means of transport for civil servants. In this regard, the government notes that 'integrated planning capacity, at both an operational (municipal) and long-term strategic planning level remain fragile. Institutional capacity in the different sectors is in broad terms low...in practice, administrations do not have the capacity to coordinate, monitor and evaluate the programmes of different implementing agencies'.[35]

At the time of the research no comprehensive baseline study of human resource capacity had been completed, but the official socio-economic profile of the province points to the existence of slightly more than 50 graduate cadres (all situated in the provincial capital) and 400 technical cadres (in all municipalities).

There are 423 schools in the province, of which 332 are of Level 1 (primary), although schools are disproportionately concentrated in the municipalities of Huambo and Caála (particularly secondary level). Even though most schools remained in a state of disrepair as a result of the war, there were 746,000 children of school-going age in 2003. Of note is the fact that only 23% of all school-aged children attended school in urban areas and only 16% in rural areas, according to statistics pertaining to the immediate post-war period in 2002.[36] In terms of professional training, the province has six training centres: one state-owned; four church-owned and one run by an NGO. According to the National Institute for Employment and Professional Training (INEFOP-Instituto Nacional do Emprego e Formação Profissional) there 327 people were trained in these centres in the first semester of 2002.

Also of interest is the data available on traditional authorities in the province. At the time of the research, the provincial government was engaged in reorganising and supporting structures of traditional authority, and in particular the old kingdoms of Bailundo, Huambo, Chingolo, Chiaca and Sambo. The table below shows a relatively structured network of traditional authorities in the province. As the government notes, "its importance [traditional authority] and potential in linking with rural communities is a function of various factors including the capacity for institutional articulation with modern authorities and its legitimacy *vis-a-vis* the population, and in particular rural communities".[37]

Fieldwork Review

During the quartering and demobilisation process, Huambo had four quartering/ gathering areas: Esfinge (Bailundo municipality), Chiteta I and II, and Chongolola (Sambo municipality). Menga, while geographically part of Kwanza Sul, was administratively and logistically managed from Huambo as well.

On 24 July 2002, according to information provided by the Joint Military Commission (JMC), a total of 10,650 UNITA combatants were in quartering areas, with 50,887 of their family members in family gathering areas. By May 2003, there were still 70,000 people waiting to be transported from the gathering areas of Chiteta, Esfinge and Sambo, while approximately 2,000 people were living in abandoned buildings in Bailundo and in other areas.

At the time of the research, the majority of these people were believed to have resettled, and NGOs and WFP had ceased to assist populations in transit – although there was little concrete data to back this up. We should note that, as was the case in other provinces, the patterns of return and resettlement early on were believed to include the maintenance by IDPs of 'dual households' – one in the city and one in a rural area. Consequently, some former IDPs, although nominally returned, had continued to 'commute' to urban areas to earn money.

Table 2: Traditional Authorities in Huambo Province[38]

Municipality	King	Great Soba	Soba	Seculo	Number of traditional authorities	State authorities	Total	Scope of Traditional Authority
Province	*5*	*166*	*375*	*1,822*	*2,368*	*132*	*2,500*	*894*
Bailundo	1	37	19	393	450	12	462	579
Caála	1	11	33	273	318	12	330	521
Cachiungo	0	16	19	122	157	12	169	483
Chicala Cholohanga	1	12	24	138	175	12	187	950
Chinjenje	1	1	7	44	53	12	65	773
Ecunha	0	5	25	177	207	12	219	435
Huambo	1	34	148	46	229	12	241	3,945
Londuimbali	0	24	14	204	242	12	254	535
Longonjo	0	8	20	122	150	12	162	760
Mungo	0	9	45	166	220	12	232	473
Ucuma	0	9	21	137	167	12	179	403

Fonte: Governo da Província do Huambo - "Informação do Governo da Província do Huambo à Comissão de Administração e Poder Local da Assembleia Nacional" de Agosto/2002

According to the official socio-economic survey of the province, the group of demobilised soldiers was mainly composed of 'rank and file' with a family averaging six people. The composite profile put forward was as follows: "it is a young population, in its productive years, wishing to resettle in a rural area, where most of them come from". [39]

Fieldwork in the province was conducted over a period of two weeks during January and February 2004. The research project was once again discussed with local authorities, including the provincial offices of the Institute for the Socio-Professional Reintegration of Ex-Military Personnel (IRSEM – *Instituto de Reinserção Sócio Económica dos Ex-Militares*), who provided critical assistance in revising and improving the methodology.

As mentioned before, Huambo city is one of the largest cities in Angola apart from Luanda. It has an estimated population of 750-900,000 people, close to half of the province's official estimated total population. [40] At the time the project personnel arrived, Huambo city was run down with no mains water supply and very weak electricity only switched on in the evening. Roads within the city were almost as badly maintained as those outside it, and the state of buildings around the city centre reflected the intensity of the fighting that took place within it. There is very little active industry and the city remains poorly connected to the coast and other major cities – the Benguela railway operates only in small stretches and the roads leading out of Huambo are dirt roads, prone to erosion in the rainy season and with regular landmine detonations.

In the city itself, key interviews were conducted with representatives of the Angolan government, including IRSEM personnel and provincial representatives of the Ministry of Reinsertion and Social Assistance (MINARS – *Ministério de Acção e Reinserção Social*). [41] In addition, project personnel interviewed several members of local and international NGOs, including the United Nations Office for the Coordination of Humanitarian Affairs (OCHA), WFP, the Agency for Rural Development and the Environment (ADRA), World Vision, Halo Trust, Okutiuka, Save the Children (UK), Caritas, and Solidarités.

Focus group discussions (and survey collection) were undertaken in the urban/peri-urban areas of Santa-Teresa and Vilinga, both located close to the centre of the city. The estimated population of Santa Teresa is 2,792, a relatively high population density for an area which has historically been sparsely populated. During the war, there were many displaced people in Santa Teresa and in the "Acumol" IDP camp nearby, but when the war ended the majority of them left. Acumol was then turned into a transit centre for demobilised soldiers, thus attracting a new influx of people. Some still remained in the camp at the time of fieldwork, but local leaders were unable to identify how many.

There was little displacement from this area during the war – a small number went to Luanda but most have since returned. There was also little population mobility during the war – it is only since 2002 that a few residents have begun to travel to other provinces to trade or to visit family. A number of NGOs were active in Santa Teresa – WFP and the International Committee of the Red Cross (ICRC) in emergency food distribution, and DW, which provided a water point.

The MPLA has a representative in the community and contact with the provincial government is mediated through periodic meetings at the local administration. At the time, there was no police presence but the civil defence force was active actively deterring crime, especially at night.

According to local leaders, community solidarity was considerably weakened by the conflict, as was the case in many other urban areas. Many customs and traditions are no longer practiced even though they were once an important part of community life – dances, other ceremonies used to mark important events such as birth, marriage, and the harvest of crops. In addition, and through a number of key interviews, project researchers got the initial impression that the traditional leader *(Soba)* – once highly respected and all-powerful – was now apparently little respected by the communities. The destruction of the social fabric during decades of civil war, the arrival of "new things and new ways" were considered the main factors in the erosion of the power of traditional leaders. Understanding the present day role of traditional authorities was incorporated as a secondary objective of the research, and the findings will be discussed in more detail below.

In Huambo, as in most provincial capitals in Angola, the distinction between urban and rural is not clear-cut – yet, efforts were made to remain as true to this distinction as possible. As the data gathered through survey collection will show, a substantial number of people in these apparently urban, built-up areas earn their livelihoods from the cultivation of land around the edges of the city, and levels of engagement in both the formal and informal non-agricultural economy are lower than might be expected in a city. This is characteristic of contemporary Angola and is an inbuilt constraint in the dataset.

While there is considerably more employment available in Huambo than in rural areas, the majority of the population works in the informal sector and many still cultivate small parcels of land, often several kilometres away from their houses. According to the Provincial Group for the Assessment of Vulnerability, Huambo's urban population's main sources of food were: market purchases (59%), food aid (22%) and own production (19%). In fact, even for the relatively more urbanised population of Huambo, relying on food aid had become a way of supplementing the meagre proceeds of their own agricultural production. Livelihood strategies mirrored this situation of dependency. As noted by the group, "in these areas, the diversity of activities used by families to guarantee their livelihoods is visible" – and they included, among others, agricultural labour (28%); sale of firewood and coal (20%); sale of miscellaneous products (28%); and sale of wild produce (14%). Commercial crops accounted for a mere 9% of total income.[42]

It should also be noted that it was considerably more difficult to locate ex-combatants in the urban/peri-urban areas of Huambo city than in the rural areas surveyed by the project. In addition, former combatants in urban/peri-urban areas seemed more reluctant to be interviewed – perhaps an inherent characteristic of urban areas where levels of anonymity are higher. The assistance of a local *Soba* as well as the local administrator was engaged to help establish contact with former combatants, making possible the gathering of a total of 95 surveys in Huambo's urban and peri-urban areas of Santa-Teresa and Vilinga. In addition, four focus group discussions were carried out with ex-combatants (broken down by age and rank); two focus groups with women community members; and, finally, an additional three interviews were conducted with local government, the *Soba,* and a local church leader.

The commune of Sambo was identified for 'rural' fieldwork in the municipality of Vila Nova (Tchicala Tcholoanga). Sambo is remote from both the provincial and municipal capitals, with difficult access and no major transport routes. It can thus be considered authentically 'rural' in the sense of offering no real economic opportunities beyond subsistence agriculture and no real major social or economic infrastructure.

Although in most municipalities, the town is also the centre point for markets, trade, transport etc, Vila Nova is roughly divided into separate areas for geographical and logistical reasons. Thus, Sambo is a particularly remote commune within Vila Nova municipality with little connection to Vila Nova town itself. Access to Sambo is dependent on road conditions and periodically blocked by bridge collapse, excessive mud, or landmines. Sambo has very little in the way of social infrastructure: the entire municipality had only 13 functioning primary schools and by November 2003 there was just a single functioning health post in the entire commune.[43]

There were an estimated 624 demobilised soldiers in Sambo at the time of research, of a total of 1,657 registered by IRSEM in the municipality of Vila Nova as a whole.[44] There had been a quartering area in Sambo, which had an estimated population of 32,000, although it has since closed. There was no concrete data on whether all the demobilised combatants had left, where they went, or how many may have remained in the area.

Ex-combatants were interviewed in Sambo during a food distribution activity and in the village of Lombundi, just outside Sambo. Most were from remote villages and had walked or come by bicycle to Sambo to collect rations.

Sambo itself (the 'town') consists of about 10 buildings, only one or two of which have a functioning roof. It has the remains of a wide avenue which appears to have been lined with streetlamps once, but now it is mostly a dirt track which runs out shortly outside Sambo. There is a minimal market, which sells charcoal and some basic foodstuffs but very little fresh produce. There is some electricity, from a generator switched on for a few hours at night only – there are few lights or electrical appliances in Sambo in any case. There is a degree of informal settlement in Sambo, predominantly rural in character – basic, hand-built houses. At the time of fieldwork there were also a number of ex-combatants housed in tents, awaiting food distribution, and two large 'marquee'-style tents functioning as warehouses for WFP food supplies.

The government maintains a presence in Sambo through the communal administrator. In addition to the government presence, UNITA has a committee in Sambo. Some members of the UNITA committee are not originally from this area – having been quartered in the Sambo quartering area they were then assigned this location by the communal administration. They did not intend to leave, having become integrated into party structures here.

Lombundi is typical of rural settlement in the central highlands – to a degree, the data gathered in Lombundi paints the average picture of 'rural' ex-combatants surveyed. Lombundi is in fact an *Ombala*, a larger grouping of five villages which fall under the traditional authority of the *'Soba Grande'* – the 'head soba' – though each village would have an individual soba, who reports to him. The population mostly lives in small, hand-built houses, occasionally with corrugated iron roofs but mostly thatched. Around these houses are small plots (called *Ocumbo*) cultivated with crops for sale and household subsistence.

Village life revolves around two places: the *Onjango*, a round building used for community meetings, and the Catholic church, which is probably the most impressive building in the village. There is no health post in Lombundi, and although the government had (at the time of the research) provided teachers, there was no school building – the church doubling up as a school. The *Sobas* attend regular meetings with the commune administration in Sambo, and there is an MPLA committee in Lombundi itself. The MPLA flag flies in the middle of the village. There is no police or army presence here or nearby, but there is a civil defence force composed of four people, who maintain order (although they are unarmed).

The entire population of this area was displaced in 1998 – some went to Huambo and some to the bush with UNITA. The *Soba* (head *soba*) only returned in July 2003, accompanied by a large number of families that had also been displaced. Many have not returned at all and the population is significantly lower than before. In addition to those who were displaced and decided not to come back, many have died. The research found a considerable number of residents who were not originally from this community – many former combatants brought back wives from different areas and there was also a small number of displaced families that had come from other areas.

Fieldwork in Sambo coincided with a WFP food distribution activity. While this enabled quick surveying of a large number of ex-combatants, it made strict random sampling impossible and included ex-combatants residing outside Sambo. However, all former combatants interviewed were resident in nearby areas with broadly the same rural characteristics. The assistance of local leaders and the administrator of Sambo were once again critical to making contact with ex-combatants.

A later visit to the province during September 2004 provided additional focus group data, particularly regarding the role of traditional ceremonies in facilitating reintegration into communities, as well as establishing a stronger sense of community perceptions of the ex-soldiers. The first interviews were held at Cantão Pahula, a small settlement (a former IDP and transit camp) along the Lubango road; as well as at the bairro of Santa Teresa and surrounding settlements. Focus group interviews were conducted not only with ex-soldiers, but also wives of ex-soldiers, community leaders, and general members of the community. Focus group discussions were supplemented with interviews of a number of 'key informants', namely individuals at the Christian Children's Fund, Okiatuka and Development Workshop (Huambo) to learn more about the traditional ceremonies and to explore their perception of the problems involved in reintegration.

Bié

Overview of the Province

Located in the eastern central plateau, Bié province benefits from one of the most important river networks in the country: the Kwanza and Cubango basins, and the Lundo, Cuemba, Cutato and Cuiva rivers. The province borders seven other Angolan provinces: Malange to the north, Lunda-Sul to the northeast, Moxico to the east, Kuando Kubango to the south, Huíla to the southwest, Huambo to the west and Kwanza-Sul to the northwest.

Bié's population is highly heterogeneous. Various ethno-linguistic groups have historically inhabited the province: the Umbundu (in all municipalities,

Map 6: Province of Bié

traditionally focused on agriculture and livestock farming as well as fishing), the Kioco (located in the east and south of the province primarily in the municipalities of Kuemba and east of Chitembo), and the Ganguela (located in the south of the province, in Chitembo municipality and south of Camacupa).

Rough population estimates (extrapolated from the latest polio vaccination campaign) pointed to approximately 1.8 million people in the province and a density of 15.6 people per square kilometre. Although this was the figure used by the provincial government at the time of the research, population figures used by Bié's Provincial Group for the Assessment of Vulnerability were much lower at 1,295,000 people.[45] The province's population is extremely young, with 55% under 20 and only 2% above the age of 65.[46] Be that as it may, one of the characteristics of this population is that it is extremely mobile – within and outside the province – as will be discussed below. Furthermore, the province has a disproportionately high number of female-headed households – close to 40%, according to MINARS.[47]

Bié was one of Angola's provinces most seriously affected by the civil war. The immediate post-independence war, the post-electoral war or 'war of the cities' (1992-1994), as well as the last phase of the war severely affected the province. Four of the province's municipalities were classified as highly mined during 2002, with one mine accident occurring per 10,000 people. From 1992 onwards, large areas of the province were isolated, particularly the areas north of Andulo and Cuemba, as well as the communes of Ringoma and Umpulo (in Camacupa municipality), part of the corridor used both by UNITA and the FAA to travel from Kuando Kubango to Moxico.

At the end of the war, 1,836 kilometres of roads, a third of which were primary roads, needed rehabilitation. In addition, and of critical importance for the reconstruction effort of the province and the country as a whole, the Benguela railway (with an extension of 360km and crossing 5 municipal capitals in Bié) required almost total rehabilitation.[48]

During the various cycles of war, a significant proportion of the province's population found refuge in and around Kuíto as well as other built-up areas. By the end of the war, the provincial capital hosted several thousand displaced people in makeshift camps, some of which were organised by municipality of origin. While the estimated number of people displaced in the province was estimated at 516,832 in 2002, data gathered *in situ* for the purposes of the government's provincial profile pointed to 384,000 displaced people in the province or 21% of the total provincial population during 2003.[49]

Since the signature of the MoU in April 2002, approximately 260,877 people had returned to the province.[50] In fact, by October 2002, close to 45,715 people had spontaneously returned, citing the beginning of the agricultural season as their main reason for returning – although exhaustion with life in displacement camps was also a main reason. During January 2004, the WFP noted that 123,049 previously displaced people had resettled, that 95,451 former combatants and their families had also resettled, but warned that 40,563 people remained internally displaced.

We should add that, as was the case throughout the country, a significant proportion of the resettlement was done without official support. In this regard, the province's socio-economic profile points to 41 out of every 100 people having returned and resettled without support (of a displaced population in 2003 of 384,000). The average size of the displaced family was calculated at 4.2 (organised resettlement) and 3.7 (spontaneous return). As in other provinces, some of the problems identified by humanitarian agencies as having delayed (and continuing to delay) the normalisation of the province include: de-mining (although many of the areas had been already mapped by INAROEE and Halo Trust – particularly around main urban areas where there was stationing of troops); the difficulty in movement of people and goods, and the lack of food, agricultural inputs and consumer goods.

The province is divided into 9 municipalities and 30 communes as can be seen in the map below.

The provincial government is composed of the governor and 2 vice-governors and their respective technical teams, as well as 12 provincial directors.[51] As in other provinces, public administration is regulated at provincial, municipal and communal level by law-decree No 17/99 of 29 October 1999 on the "Administrative Reform of the State" as well as Decree No 27/00 of 19 May 2000 that provides the regulatory framework of provincial government and municipal and communal administrations.

Map 7: Province of Bié: Municipalities

Table 3: Provincial Government: Organogram[52]

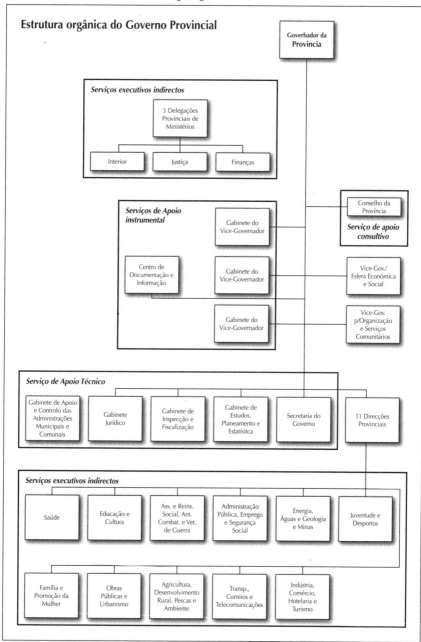

The functional extension of state administration to the whole territory of the province – considered by the government a 'remarkable effort' – was still in its infancy in early 2004. Although state administration had been established in all 9 municipalities and 30 communes it suffered, as was the case in Huambo Province, from very low institutional capacity in the different sectors – a consequence of lack of capacity and human resources, dilapidated infrastructure, lack of appropriate means of transport for civil servants (in particular at municipal and communal levels), amongst others.[53] According to the government, "the capacity for integrated planning, both operational (municipal) and of a more long-term developmental strategy (provincial) is very weak (…) in addition, mechanisms for evaluating the feasibility of sector projects and (based on these) the development and coordination of integrated development plans for the province were not in place".[54]

The situation found at the time of the research was one characterised by lack of organisational capacity and coordination between government structures at provincial level and its partners – a situation made worse by the lack of reliable socio-economic data with which adequate interventions could be designed. This specifically affected the resettlement and return process – returnees were often faced with no support at the local level, no chance of employment, and therefore no means of survival. Difficulties as regards access were also critical– a function of landmine infestation, climatic conditions (heavy rains), as well as the large number of bridges and roads which remained unusable.

The provision of education in Bié was also precarious. Although there were 297 registered schools and other education facilities in the province, two-thirds of these functioned under severe difficulties. In rural areas, there was an average of 81 students per class while in urban areas there was an average of 327 students per class. According to government data there were 2,967 teachers in the province in 2003, the majority of which taught at a primary school (level I). As regards high school (Level II), the situation was very difficult because of an average of 72 students per teacher – partly explained by the influx of returnees to the urban areas. Moreover, and although there are no appropriate statistics on success rates in schools, it seems that a significant proportion of students who enrol in primary education in Bié eventually abandon school. [55]

Although conservative estimates pointed to 506,000 potential students, only 240,000 were officially registered – i.e. 60 in every 100 pupils are not registered.[56] On a positive note, the National Institute for Employment and Professional Training (INEFOP – *Instituto Nacional do Emprego e Formação Profissional*) was present in the provincial capital, and was tasked with the implementation of the government's *"Estamos Contigo"* training programme. INEFOP continued to provide short-term courses (usually lasting eight months) focusing on carpentry, construction and tailoring. With an average of 64 students for every 8-month term, it played a vital role in the province.

There are 77 health units in the province, the majority of which are health posts, which were largely destroyed during the war. At the time of the research, there were two private clinics and three pharmacies in Kuito, and the majority of health-related infrastructure was situated in the provincial capital. During 2003, there were only 12 doctors in the province (3 Angolans and 9 foreigners) – an average of 1 doctor for 35,321 people, 1 nurse per 2,315 people (urban areas) and 1 per 5,133 people (rural areas). We should note that during 2003 there wasn't a single doctor in the rural areas.[57] As noted by the government, the total volume of public expenditure allocated to health was very low – in 2000 *per capita* expenditure on health in the province was estimated at US$2 (or US$6 including support by donors).[58]

The people and organisations cited above were ill-equipped to deal with the health situation in the province. According to *Médecins sans Frontières* (MSF – Spain) in Kuíto, malaria, tuberculosis and *pellagra* continued to kill several thousand people every year. When the project arrived in Kuito (February 20094), MSF was still concerned about communities that had yet to be reached by the humanitarian community (such as in Ringoma and Umpulo), as well as with a number of areas that were not accessible at that moment (Mutumbo, Cambandua).[59]

Bié province is predominantly rural, with the majority of its population depending on an agricultural system that revolves around the production of maize. When the project arrived in the province, livelihood strategies tended to vary according to whether the people in question were residents, displaced or had just resettled or returned. As noted by the Provincial Group for the Assessment of Vulnerability, "opportunity for alternative income generating activities did not fundamentally change during the period [November 2003 to April 2004], but there are significant differences in income-generating strategies between returnees and residents". This can be seen in the graph below:

The resident population (*'residentes'*) obtained its income primarily from agriculture and commerce (trading mainly in agricultural produce, but also

Graph 2: Sources of Income in Bié by returned and resident populations[60]

in a variety of consumer goods), using the thriving local informal economy.[61] As can be seen in the graph above, these are, by order of importance as sources of income for the resident population: sale of firewood and coal ('*venda lenha e* carvão'), sale of surplus produce ('*venda excedentes de produção*'), sale of beverages ('*venda bebidas caseiras*'), sale of livestock ('*venda animais*') and agricultural labour ('*empreitada* agrícola').

Within the displaced and recently returned and resettled populations, the main source of food was provided by humanitarian agencies, roughly three times the amount obtained through the residents' own production and market purchases. [62] Nevertheless, we should note that a series of rapid diagnosis exercises conducted in the province revealed that there had been a general improvement in the situation with a decrease in importance of food aid and an increase in the production ability of returnees.[63] Similar to the situation found in Huambo, the main sources of income for returnees were, by order of importance, agricultural labour, sale of firewood and coal, sale of surplus produce and sale of livestock.

In order to better monitor the population's vulnerability, the province was divided into four distinct regions – defined on the basis of their situation as regards agriculture and trade as well as households' recovery capacity. During 2003, the majority of areas in the province were considered 'moderate' or 'moderate to low' risk (32 communes of a total of 39), while 7 communes were considered to be in a 'low risk' situation. At the end of

Map 8: Bié's Agriculture and Trade Recovery Regions

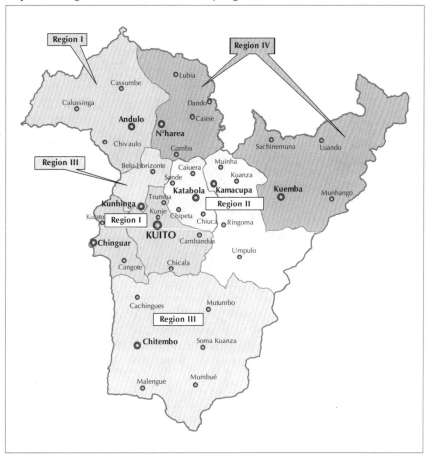

2003, of the four regions detailed in the map below, two were considered to be on a steady and rapid course to recovery.[64]

Region I (light green in the map) has experienced a fast and sustained recovery of its trade networks due to its links to Huambo, with a very dynamic local trade economy spreading from Kuíto to the rest of the province. In addition, region I has two centres of agricultural development: Andulo and Chinguar. Region II, to the northeast of Kuíto and incorporating the municipalities of Catabola and Camacupa, was considered to be recovering at a steady pace – Camacupa, in particular, has experienced a considerable influx of migrant workers looking for jobs in alluvial diamond exploration.

Region III on the other hand, incorporating Cunhinga and Chitembo, has experienced a slower pace of recovery, mostly as a result of difficult and, in some instances impossible, access. Both municipalities were still heavily dependent on humanitarian assistance at the time the project arrived in the province. Finally, Region IV (which incorporates the municipalities of Nharea and Cuemba) has experienced serious obstacles to its recovery – both as regards trade as well as agricultural production. Problems of accessibility, particularly in the rainy season, rendered vast areas of this region inaccessible. Heavily dependent on the other regions for the provision of food and other items, Region IV remained in a precarious situation at the time of fieldwork. In addition, the lack of a monetary economy in large tracts of this region, has inhibited trade and the establishment of permanent markets, and has artificially inflated prices of all items.

Overall, the Vulnerability Assessment Provincial Group considered that the areas experiencing a faster pace of recovery were (in order of importance): (1) Chinguar, Kuito and Andulo; (2) Catabola and Camacupa, (3) Cunhinga and Chitembo; and finally, (4) Nharea and Cuemba. By May 2004, the situation in the province had in fact improved, with 11 communes considered in moderate risk and 14 in 'moderate to low' risk.[65]

Nevertheless, households of returnees were still experiencing a relatively high level of vulnerability, particularly due to the end of food stocks from the previous agricultural season as well as because of an observed increase in prices of products which constitute the typical food basket. Although the situation in the province improved when humanitarian agencies began to reach previously inaccessible areas, during the first months of 2004, 40,000 families (or 150,000-200,000) people still remained out of reach.[66] The Provincial Group's Assessment of Vulnerability provided a slightly lower figure showing that 135,800 people were still vulnerable to food insecurity in April 2004 (of which 10,600 were food insecure; 49,600 highly vulnerable; 58,000 moderately vulnerable and 17,600 potentially vulnerable).[67]

The resilience of the province's population was emphasised by MINARS in the following terms:

> ...Bié's rural population is well adapted to the environmental conditions of its traditional settlement areas as well as those of resettlement areas. With the means available to it, this population has a strong capacity to deal with difficult circumstances. Only this explains the fact that both resettled populations as well as those that found refuge in the surrounding woods are rebuilding their villages

and their economic activities often without any support from the outside. This factor represents the greatest potentiality as regards the social reintegration and economic and productive re-organisation of rural communities and the economy of the Province.[68]

On the whole, the province has good agricultural potential and is expected to become one of the country's main suppliers of grain– in fact, it should be recalled that before independence, the province was the largest producer of rice in Angola. Bié's large flood plains and abundance of water make agriculture a viable option. Several of the key interviewees highlighted that the creation of socio-economic opportunities in the province will have to be based, in the short and medium term, on agriculture. The granting of land, 'rural extension' policies and training in basic agricultural techniques are crucial in this regard, as is the rehabilitation of infrastructure.

Bié presents ideal conditions for the cultivation of maize, beans, rice, manioc, peanut, wheat, potatoes as well as coffee and several types of fruit trees. According to the provincial government, 239,000 families occupied an area estimated at 965,000 hectares during 2003 – an average of 4 hectares per family.[69] At that time, there were approximately 10,800 commercial farmers occupying 14% of arable land with an average plot size of 14 hectares. While the yields of the province's two main crops (corn and beans) are low among subsistence farmers, it is 2.5 times higher for corn and 4 times higher for beans in the commercial sector. At the time of the survey, a single agricultural engineer and two veterinary doctors covered the whole of the province, with an average of one agricultural technician per 3,625 families. This average was subject to severe distortion at local level: in Andulo, for example, there was one agriculture technician for 37,768 families.

The development of the province's agricultural sector faced a number of limitations, some of which were highlighted by the government. They included a severe shortage of agricultural technicians and their asymmetric distribution across the province (as well as their low motivation due to very low/unpaid salaries); absence of adequate means of transport; severe degradation of roads and high levels of mine infestation; the destruction of support infrastructure (such as warehouses), and finally, the lack of financial support for rural rehabilitation.[70]

During 2004, the province had just a single commercial bank in the provincial capital. In terms of industry, there are 100 small enterprises registered, of which 87 are located in the provincial capital but a third of them are not operating. Most of these are small businesses such as bakeries or carpentry workshops. The trade network is composed of 118 registered establishments, of which 318 are retailers; 118 are of a mixed character and 161 are based in the rural areas. There are 20 rural markets across the province and 9 urban markets. There is one commercial establishment per 7,400 people in urban areas and 25,900 in rural areas.

There are 27 NGOs and 3 churches that are actively working in urban and peri-urban areas, mostly in social and humanitarian projects. In the immediate post-war period, these agencies played a critical role in emergency support to the province's thousands of displaced people (particularly in the areas of health and nutrition, education and training, agriculture and food security).[71]

In terms of traditional authorities, it is worthwhile citing the socio-economic profile of the province: 'similarly to what is happening in the rest of the country, the province is undergoing a process to support the re-organisation of structures of traditional authority, of recovering the dignity and important social role of traditional authorities in the rural areas'. Numbers of traditional authorities in province are not provided however – a fact that the government attributes to the displacement that occurred as a result of the war.[72]

Fieldwork Review

During the quartering and demobilisation process, Bié had three quartering/gathering areas: Ngamba I, Ngamba II and N'Dele. During July 2002, according to information provided by the Joint Military Commission (JMC), a total of 5,863 UNITA combatants were in quartering areas, with 19,407 of their family members in family reception areas. By May 2003, all quartering areas had been officially closed and their populations moved to make-shift camps (old schools, an old Catholic mission, and tents in Andulo, for example) or resettled somewhere else in the province.

Nevertheless, as in Huambo and Huíla provinces, the number of demobilised soldiers officially registered[73] was much higher than the JMC figure above – during September 2003 a total of 19,733 former combatants and 61,058 of their family members had registered, a substantially higher number than at the time of demobilisation.[74]

Project personnel returned to Angola to carry out fieldwork in Bié province in February 2004. Following the experience in Huambo, the team decided to conduct survey collection and interviews in two municipalities: Andulo (within it, Andulo commune) and Kuíto city (within it, Cunge and Cuemba communes).

For a number of practical reasons, the project team decided to begin its work in the province in Andulo municipality. Interviews held in Kuíto had highlighted the fact that more than half the demobilised soldiers in the province had resettled in Andulo. It had also emerged that, for the first time since the war had ended, former combatants resettled in the municipality were being assisted with the distribution of agricultural tools and seeds by a number of humanitarian agencies. These activities resulted in a high concentration of former combatants in the centre of town during the time the project spent in Andulo, making the collection of surveys easier.[75]

To the north and northwest of Kuíto city, Andulo municipality, and within it Andulo town, were pivotal in UNITA's war efforts in the province. In fact, for several years Jonas Savimbi kept a base in Andulo – its location allowing for the coordination of repeated offensives by UNITA on Kuíto city. The whole municipality, and in particular the town, carries deep scars from the years of war, and the few buildings still standing bear evidence of the

Table 4: Population data for Kuíto and Andulo municipalities[76]

Municipality	Commune	Population total	Population density
Kuíto	Kuíto	263,172	44
	Trumba	9,279	11
	Cambândua	16,943	18
	Chicala	13,187	9
	Cunje	35,576	32
	Total	**338,157**	**33**
Andulo	Andulo	102,621	10
	Chivaulo	49,473	24
	Cassumbe	20,123	5
	Calussinga	33,319	15
	Total	**205,536**	**11**

ferocity of combat in the area. Only 20 houses had electricity at the time of the research.

Andulo municipality remained highly mined, with 11 mine accidents registered in 2003 alone. Only after the war ended were humanitarian agencies able to assess the situation here, which was largely unknown to either the government or the humanitarian community. Socio-economic data for the municipality was either out of date or unreliable – for example, population statistics for the municipality dated from 1992 (188,841) while humanitarian agencies used an estimate of 205,536, as can be seen in the table below. Government data shows 23% of the people in the municipality were displaced.

This data also highlights that the municipality has one of the lowest levels of school enrolment, with a troubling 12.9% schooling rate. In 2003, only two NGOs worked in the municipality, a number that grew during 2004 and 2005.

On a positive note, the municipality had one of the highest numbers of registered commercial farmers (3,510), a distinction the municipality shared with Chinguar and Kunhinga. Needless to say, production was severely affected in all areas of economic life: the municipality had virtually no (light) industry left, with just a single bakery operating in town. The commercial network offered more prospects and, in particular, Andulo's three rural markets continued to play a vital role for its residents.

A total of 153 former combatants were surveyed and several key informant interviews and focus group discussions were conducted. Among those interviewed were Andulo's Deputy Administrator, the Municipal Secretary of UNITA and the *Soba* of Chivili commune. Focus-group discussions were held with a group of recently demobilised high-ranking officers from UNITA; with community leaders; with a group of demobilised soldiers; and, finally, with a group of teenagers.

The team then returned to Kuíto city to conduct research in Cunge and Cuemba communes. The centre of the city of Kuíto was in complete ruins, having been the scene of intense fighting for several years. During the war, the centre of town had been under FAA control. UNITA had surrounded the city for long periods and the government reacted by creating an 'aerial bridge' to support the embattled FAA forces.

Jonas Savimbi's forces tried repeatedly to occupy the town from his base in Andulo, just two hours away. Many of the residents still found it hard to explain how a comparatively small FAA garrison was able to resist UNITA's attacks, particularly those headed by General Bock, who mounted a devastating offensive in December 1998. Evidence of this offensive is still visible along the road to Andulo. For many, UNITA's defeat at Kuito signalled a reversal in the fortunes of the movement. The October 1999 offensive by the FAA (termed locally 'the nine-month war') would put an end to UNITA's presence in Andulo and Bailundo, forcing the movement to move east in the province and towards Moxico.

Local traditional authorities were contacted in Cunge and their assistance in the identification and gathering of former combatants in their areas requested. As in Huambo, locating large numbers of ex-combatants was considerably more difficult in Cunge, and the team relied heavily on the assistance of traditional leaders. As a result, the number of surveys collected was considerably lower, at 55. The project also focused on semi-structured interviews with a number of key agencies and organisations present in the provincial capital. Key informant interviews were conducted with the ICRC, MSF, the WFP and INEFOP (National Institute for Employment and Professional Training). In addition, a number of focus group discussions were also undertaken with a group of *Sobas* and a group of female soldiers.

Huíla

Overview of the Province

With an area of 79,022 square kilometres, Huíla Province is situated in the southwest of the country. It borders six other provinces: Namibe and Benguela to the west; Benguela and Huambo to the north; Bié and Cuando-Cubango to the east and, finally, Cunene to the South.

An estimated 3,012,621 people inhabited Huíla Province in 2002, 46% of whom were urban-based.[77] Huíla's ethno-linguistic make-up is markedly diverse: six main ethno-linguistic groups are present, including Nyaneca-Nkhumbi, Umbundu, Nganguela, Quioco, Herero and non-Bantu groups.

The province comprises 14 municipalities and 65 communes, and provincial administration is structured along the same lines as the other two provinces, the same legislation applying. Unlike the two other provinces surveyed, administrative structures at the level of the provincial capital (Lubango) remained largely functional throughout the conflict. Part of the reason for this was that Lubango was not as directly affected by the conflict as the other urban sites chosen for survey research. An additional factor, emphasised in the province's socio-economic profile, is the fact that the province retained a significant training and education infrastructure, which strengthened its ability (to the degree possible in war) to plan, manage and implement programmes. In contrast to Bié for example, the provincial administration had a younger workforce educated at technical and university levels, and administration buildings were relatively well preserved in the provincial capital. [78]

Yet, while this may have been the case as regards Lubango and its environs, the establishment of adequate functional links between the provincial level and municipal levels remained highly challenging.[79] The government had initiated the extension of central administration to many of Huíla's municipalities some years before the end of the war, but local administration remained particularly weak (or non-existent) at the time of the research in some of the northern and north-eastern municipalities where the war had been more intense.[80]

By the end of the war, displacement in Huíla was considerable; OCHA's figures for September 2002 pointed to a total of 191,000 displaced while MINARS had registered 315,941 displaced people, of which 71,149 were being assisted during the last quarter of 2002. The largest number of displaced people was located in the municipalities of Chipindo, Kuvango, Quilengues and Caconda.

There is no doubt that the significant variations in Huila's population were direct consequences of the civil war. Although statistical information must be used cautiously, it is significant that its population grew from an estimated 1,137,475 in 1995 to an estimated 3,012,621 in 2002. This exponential growth was significantly more pronounced in urban areas (and in particular Lubango) where, in a mere seven years, an estimated 1,195,183 additional people sought refuge. In Chipindo the population would increase threefold between 1995 and 2002; from an estimated 17,792 people to 57,705 by 2002.[81]

While the war deeply affected the province's socio-economic fabric (including structures of traditional authority) as a whole, Huila's northern and eastern municipalities were the hardest hit. During the emergency phase, a large number of UN system organisations were present in the province, including the WFP, UNICEF, OCHA, FAO and UNDP. In addition, a number of religious institutions play a significant role in the provision of humanitarian assistance: the Catholic Church, the *Igreja Evangélica do Sinodal de Angola* (IESA), etc.

Having experienced similar patterns of irregular and heavy rainfall during the rainy season of 2003/2004, and although less affected then the other two provinces, certain of Huíla's municipalities lost up to 70% of their agricultural production. The effects on accessibility were perhaps more seriously: large areas in the north and east became difficult to reach (and at times inaccessible) from November 2003 to April 2004.

The provincial group that monitors vulnerability to food insecurity considered that the province did not present serious problems (partly because of a relatively good harvest and good cereal reserves from previous years), but the municipalities of Caconda, Chipindo, Kuvango and Quilengues were particularly affected and required food aid throughout the period. In Chipindo, for example, 19% of people's sources of food were provided through food aid. Overall, the province had 130,330 people in a situation of vulnerability: 31,770 of whom were food insecure; 29,630 faced high vulnerability; 45,800 moderate vulnerability and 23,130 considered potentially vulnerable.[82]

With the exception of the northwest of the province (municipality of Quilengues) Huíla has an average altitude of 1,000 meters above sea level. The province benefits from two significant river basins, the Cunene and Cubango rivers, and is divided into five main agricultural zones. The northern municipalities (Caluquembe, Caconda, Chiconda and Chipindo) are predominantly maize cultivation areas, a function of irregular patterns of rainfall. The central and eastern municipalities (Matal, Quipungo and the north-west of Jamba and Chibia) are characterised by a combination of farming (of a wide variety of crops) and herding. The southern zone (the municipalities of Chibia, Gambos and the southern parts of Quipungo and matala) has a lower rainfall average and is primarily dedicated to herding. The municipalities of Humpata, Lubango, Cacula and northern Chibia form part of what is known as the 'Huila highlands'. Finally, the municipalities of Quilengues and the north-west of Cacula form part of Agriculture zone 27.[83]

Agricultural production has declined markedly over the past 25 years. During the research period the province continued to be heavily dependent on WFP assistance and imports. There were approximately 210,930 families devoted to farming, cultivating an area of close to 244,538ha. For the purposes of planning, the government divided the agricultural sector into three components: a traditional sector (formed by non-associated farmers), a sector formed by farmers who are organised into associations and, finally, a small private sector geared for commercial agriculture and cattle farming, which is gaining increased importance.[84] Cattle farming is a critical economic sector in the province, making Huíla a leader in this kind of economic activity countrywide. It has considerable potential.

The traditional sector is by far the largest and is includes approximately 80% of all farmers in the province – estimated at 210,930. Since the techniques applied are rudimentary and agricultural inputs very scarce, this is also a sector characterised by a high degree of vulnerability. Within the 20% represented by the "organised farmers'" sector, it is interesting to note that 628 farmers associations exist in the province – comprising 35,591 members, of which 50% are women. Yet, 'the majority of these farmers continue to use traditional farming methods as a result of the lack of 'inputs' and technical support'.[85] Also of note is the higher average plot size when compared to other provinces. The Huíla average is 2.3 hectares per family, varying from 1 to 3.5 hectares.[86]

The commercial sector is formed by a small number of private farms situated along the peri-urban areas of the larger built-up areas, and also by a growing number of large commercial farms dedicated to cattle breeding. The granting of large areas to private individuals (most from Angola's economic, political and military elites) has, in the past decade, caused a strong local resentment, particularly from pastoral communities in the south of the province, in the municipality of Gambos.

Since the end of the war, trade has boomed in the provincial capital, largely a result of the province's proximity to Namibia and its strategic location at the beginning of Angola's central plateau. During the second quarter of 2002, an estimated 132 businesses were registered (wholesale and retail) and an estimated 9,800 informal traders operated in the province. One of the provincial government's priorities has been to strengthen the industrial base of the province. In addition, the tourism sector (essentially in the city of Lubango and Humpata municipality) offers considerable potential and it is expected that government efforts in this regard will be developed in the near future – perhaps returning the province to the days when, as a result of its average altitude and temperate climate, Lubango was the holiday destination of choice within the country.

Lubango has five commercial banks and a vibrant associative movement – in this regard too the provincial capital stands apart from both Huambo and Kuíto.[87] Three large professional association bodies are registered in the province, in addition to several economic development programmes specifically focused on agriculture and cattle farming. The Social Support Fund (FAS, *Fundo de Acção Social*) is present, as is the Reconstruction

Support Programme (PAR, *Programa de Apoio à Reconstrução*) financed by the European Union. FAS and PAR are pivotal in the reconstruction of infra-structure, water and sanitation facilities, and social development interventions in the province. The Community Rehabilitation and National Reconciliation Programme funded by the UNDP was also operating in the municipalities of Cacula, Quipungo and Matala. There are five commercial banks in the provincial capital.

At the time the project arrived in Huíla, it found the education there similar to that in other central plateau provinces. The displacement of thousands of civilians in several waves of migration, the destruction of infrastructure during the years of war, the lack of sufficient and properly trained teachers, and severe shortages of materials and adequate curricula, have left the province in a dire situation.

The province has six professional training centres, four technical colleges ('*institutos médios*') and four higher education faculties.[88] University level education is provided by the Higher Institute for Education (ISCED - *Instituto Superior de Ciências da Educação*) and the *Universidade Agostinho Neto* (Law and Economics) in Lubango. Technical college education in the field of health is provided by the *Escola Técnica de Saúde* (training of nurses and laboratory technicians) and in the field of tourism at the *Escola Profissional de Hotelaria e Turismo*. We should note, however, that these are all based in Lubango and Humpata.[89]

Of relevance to this study is the fact that of the 330,000 students enrolled in basic level education (*nível* I), only 8.7% continue to level II. The socio-economic profile reveals very low levels of performance, high drop-out levels, and a general lack of morale by students and teachers across the province.[90] Chipindo and Kuvango municipalities are hardest hit and have the lowest rates of schooling of all municipalities in the province.

Healthcare across the province is also extremely poor. During 2003, there was one hospital bed per 3,000 people, one nurse per 2,430, and one doctor for every 83,000. As noted by the government, the situation is far worse in rural areas. Of the seven hospitals in the province, five are located in Lubango, one in Matala, and one in Cacula.

According to data provided by the provincial government (see table below), there were 1,611 traditional authorities in the province. As noted earlier, their historical role was focused on the management of the community's day-to-day business (for example, land allocation) as well as the resolution of disputes and conflicts (over land, over inheritance, matrimonial issues, etc). With regard to traditional authorities, Huíla presents us with a slightly different picture, and one which needs additional research. As observed *in situ* by the authors on previous visits to the south/southwest of the province (particularly the municipality of Gambos) as well as noted in the province's socio-economic profile:

> In the central and southern areas, where the conflict was less pronounced, it is still possible to find unaltered traditional authority structures. The figure of the King (ohamba) represents the highest

Table 5: Traditional Authorities in Huíla Province, 2001[91]

Municipality	Great soba	Sobas	Adjunct great soba	Adjunct soba	Sekulus	Total
Lubango	4	42			122	**168**
Humpata	14	16	14	16	28	**88**
Chibia	2	24	1	5	54	**86**
Gambos*	3	21			65	**89**
Quipungo	9	9		122	69	**209**
Matala	9	24		55	124	**212**
Jamba	25	64		39	50	**178**
Kuvango	11	7			63	**81**
Chipindo	7	7			16	**30**
Caconda	13	25			92	**130**
Chicomba	12	13			32	**57**
Caluquembe	6	26			128	**160**
Quilengues	22	10			34	**66**
Cacula	4	14		14	25	**57**
Total	**141**	**302**	**15**	**251**	**902**	**1,611**

Adapted from Gabinete de Apoio e Controle das Administrações Municipais e Comunais, Huíla, 2001 as cited in Republica de Angola, Huila – Perfil Socio-Economico, Abril 2003, p. 13.

authority, responsible for and the guardian of traditional culture. He represents his people in relations with state structures and neighbouring communities; reconciles interests; and, helps solve key issues such as inter-ethnic conflicts, land related conflicts and others. Below the King there is the figure of the Soba and below that that of the Sekulu. The Soba and the Sekulu are both representatives of the King, manage the community's territory and preside over traditional courts (...) Gambos municipality is the only one that has a King, which is included in the category of Great Soba (Soba Grande). [92]

Fieldwork Review

The team conducted fieldwork in Huíla province in March and April 2004. As with the two previous provinces, an urban/peri-urban commune in the provincial capital (Lubango) and a predominantly rural municipality, that of Chipindo, were chosen as research sites.

During the quartering and demobilisation process, Huíla province had three quartering/gathering areas: Ngalangue I, II and III. On 24 July 2002, 5,233 UNITA combatants were in quartering areas with 22,585 of their family members in family reception areas.[93] In addition, 12,000 former combatants were demobilised during the Bicesse process and 4,750 during the Lusaka process. At the time the research was conducted, data on actual numbers of former combatants in the province provided by the Provincial Secretary of UNITA pointed to a total of 7,892 former combatants registered with the provincial government.

From 6 April to 13 April, the team conducted survey research, focus group discussions and interviews in Lubango, in "Sede" commune. Lubango straddles a major railroad line to the coast as well as a north-south road and has managed to hang onto its relative prosperity despite having to host thousands of IDPs during the worst years of the war. As mentioned above, the provincial capital has the highest population density (46.9%) in the province. Lubango's 450 people per square kilometre stands in sharp contrast to the average of 38 people per square kilometre in the province as a whole.[94]

In comparison to the other two provincial capitals (Bié and Huambo), Lubango retained more of its socio-economic infrastructure. Although fighting did not destroy them, the city's hospitals, schools and administrative buildings were in need of urgent repair. Yet, the indirect costs of hosting thousands of IDPs from within and outside the province, coupled with years of lack of investment took its toll on the city's infrastructure. Lubango's water and sanitation infrastructure is largely in ruins (it is more than 70 years old), with only 10% of the city's population having access to drinking water.

In Lubango, the project collected 126 surveys and held 6 focus group discussions with ex-combatants, community members and local leaders. The research team then travelled to Chipindo, in the north-east of the province. At the time the project was undertaken, Chipindo municipality, a rural area 456 kilometres from the provincial capital was home to an estimated 48,000 inhabitants. Situated within an area hotly contested during the conflict, and controlled by UNITA for several years prior to the end of the war, Chipindo had only recently experienced the arrival of government administration on 17 March 2002.

At that time, Chipindo was (in)famously described by MSF as one of the country's 'grey areas' – a place that had been inaccessible to humanitarian relief operations for several years due to a combination of high insecurity, poor road conditions, and mine infestation. In addition, the forced displacement of civilians caused by military tactics applied by both sides (so-called 'scorched-earth tactics'), coupled with the inability of a large number of relief agencies to negotiate access to civilians in those areas, contributed to a critical humanitarian situation. In fact, this situation affected a large part of the province, particularly the areas east of the line between Caluquembe and Matala.

During 2002, Chipindo experienced the worst of the immediate post-war humanitarian crisis with very high levels of disease and mortality. At that point it 'housed' 27,624 people in IDP camps. As the FAA advanced east between September 2001 and March 2002, around 18,000 people were forcibly moved from previously UNITA-controlled villages to Chipindo municipality and then 'housed' in make-shift IDP camps. The catastrophic situation created by these forced movements was so serious that, according to MSF-Spain, during April 2002, 90 people died every day in Chipindo's IDP camps. A nutritional survey among children indicated that more than a quarter of them were suffering from severe malnutrition and a further 18% from moderate malnutrition. The setting up by MSF of a therapeutic feeding centre in Chipindo in May of the same year, and the opening of supplementary feeding centres in the quartering areas of Ngalangue II and III as well at Dongo and Chilembo, drastically reduced mortality rates in the area.[95]

In addition, it should be pointed out that after the end of the war, this part of Huíla province experienced significant return movements. In fact, resettlement programmes targeting a staggering 98,000 people were underway during the second half? of 2002.

Access to Chipindo by the research team proved to be somewhat difficult, partly because of the rainy season, extremely bad road conditions, as well as mine infestation. Huíla's road infrastructure was in as bad a shape as the other two provinces surveyed. In its 2002/2003 estimates, the provincial government noted that 400 kilometres of primary roads and 630 kilometres of secondary and tertiary roads were in need of total rehabilitation.

Chipindo's infrastructure was virtually destroyed and at the time of the research there was just a very basic administrative structure and a central health post. People in Chipindo were still very poor, with few employment opportunities and signs of malnutrition and other accompanying diseases. The team was nonetheless able to conduct a significant number of surveys and key informant interviews. In all, 77 surveys were collected and five focus group discussions held, including middle/lower ranking officers as well as female ex-combatants. Amongst the key interviews conducted were one with the administrator of Chipindo; ACF; ZOA; the secretary of UNITA (Chipindo); a UNITA municipal representative (Lubango); and UNITA's provincial secretary.

CHAPTER 2
UNITA'S DEMOBILISED SOLDIERS
Portrait of the Post-Luena Target Group

Composite Portrait

This survey was conducted in both rural and urban settings across three provincial target areas. In total, 603 ex-combatants were interviewed, of which 208 were in Bié, 193 in Huambo and 202 in Huíla; with a slight preponderance of rural respondents, especially in Bié, over that of urban (see below). A total of 17 focus group meetings were held with ex-combatants and 9 with community members. In addition, 16 key informant interviews were conducted with local leaders and government representatives, NGO staff and civil society representatives. Whenever possible, and for the purposes of obtaining a clear portrait of the 'average' post-Luena ex-combatant, and to gain an understanding of the challenges and constraints to reintegration in the three provinces, the project team combined the findings from all areas surveyed. What follows is an overview of the data gathered.

Box 1: Composite Portrait of a Former UNITA Combatant

> The general portrait of the ex-UNITA combatant that emerges from this study is that of a 36-year-old male, Umbundu speaker who is married and the head of a household of approximately nine people.
>
> He is more than likely (54.7%) to earn his primary source of income through agriculture, though this is supplemented through his spouse's earning in trade as well as casual labour. Although his education level does not exceed primary schooling, military life in UNITA provided some form of vocational training for him and at least a third of his fellow soldiers. At the time of demobilisation, this ex-combatant probably held a rank ranging between private and lieutenant.
>
> He has (61%) decided to resettle near his place of birth and/or where he has familial ties. He is not typically a member of any organisation, but he does attend a church. He spends most of his time with family and perhaps with some friends.
>
> After two years of formal peace, the ex-combatant sees himself as a civilian, though almost half his comrades do not share this sentiment. And, finally, he believes that he is, along with the vast majority (90%) of his fellow demobilised soldiers, well-received by the local community.

Table 6: Surveys, Focus Groups and Key Informant Interviews Conducted

Province	Municipality	Surveys	Focus groups with ex-combatants	Focus groups with community members	Key interviews with local leaders
Bié	Kuíto	56	1	2	2
	Andulo	152	2	1	3
Huambo	Huambo	95	4	2	2
	Vila Nova	98	6	1	3
Huíla	Lubango	126	2	1	3
	Chipindo	76	2	2	3
Total		**603**	**17**	**9**	**16**

Location and number of interviews

Since no reliable data was available beforehand about the location of ex-combatants, statistical sampling could not be used. As a result, the project used a convenience sampling approach (non-probability sample design), which was felt to be appropriate because of the control provided by the fact that the population was well identified. As noted above, fieldwork was divided between urban and rural areas in three provinces, with as close to equal numbers in each as possible. The number of surveys, focus groups and key interviews conducted by municipality are detailed below:

Age

The average (mean) age of the ex-combatants was 36.5 years (median 36), with a range of 18-78. Since these surveys were done around 18 months after demobilisation, and two years after the end of the war, it is probable that the average age upon demobilisation was slightly younger.

Gender

he vast majority of respondents were male (95.2%), reflecting the overall predominance of men in the target group. Very few women were registered

Graph 3: Age of ex-combatants surveyed

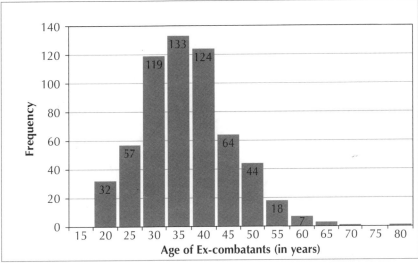

as combatants, the majority being registered as family members. However, it is probable that many women who were not demobilised – and therefore not included in the survey – were 'combatants' in the broader sense: travelling with UNITA forces and providing rear support as cooks, porters, and so on. It is also probable that women face at least the same level of difficulty in reintegration as officially registered ex-combatants, which makes it unfortunate that they could not be given more attention in our survey. Where possible, some focus groups with UNITA women were carried out.

Table 7: Gender of ex-combatants surveyed

Gender	Frequency	Percent
Male	574	95.2
Female	29	4.8
Total	**603**	**100.0**

Maternal language & other languages spoken

Almost all respondents (96%) were native Umbundu speakers; Kimbundu and Nganguela being the most common other responses. The range was broad, however, and included Kikongo, Lingala, Mumuila, Tchokwe, and Nhaneca.

It should be noted that in the majority of cases, the survey was conducted in the respondent's native language, which was usually? Umbundu. As regards other languages, 73% claimed to speak Portuguese in addition to their maternal language, while only 22% spoke no second language. The other most commonly spoken languages were Nganguela, Tchokwe and Kimbundu. There were also a few English and French speakers.

There was little difference between the genders, with only 1 woman (out of 29) who was not a native Umbundu speaker. In addition, the proportion of women claiming to speak Portuguese was actually higher than among the men, at 79%, and the number speaking no second language was lower, at 17%.

Literacy/education levels

As shown in the table below, over half the ex-combatants surveyed had not progressed beyond the first level of primary school education, and only a small minority (7% for men, 10% for women) had reached the third level or above – a proportion only slightly higher than those claiming to be illiterate.

Table 8: Resettlement locations

| Level of education | Gender of interviewee | | | |
| | Male | | Female | |
	Frequency	Percent	Frequency	Percent
1st level schooling	361	62.9%	15	51.7%
2nd level schooling	140	24.4%	9	31.0%
3rd level schooling	36	6.3%	2	6.9%
'medio'	4	0.7%	1	3.4%
illiterate	31	5.4%	2	6.9%
data missing	2	0.3%	0	0.0%
Total	574	100.0%	29	100.0%

As will be discussed below, the lack of qualifications constitutes the single most important obstacle to finding formal employment, in an environment with very high rates of unemployment.[96] In this regard, the assessment of functional literacy for those who claim to have formal education, although outside of the scope of this project, is also a priority.

The majority of interviewees chose to resettle in the place in which they were born, or less commonly, where they had previously lived. In fact, 79.4% had resettled, even if not in the village or *bairro* of their birth, at least in the same province. Just one fifth chose to resettle in a place where they had never lived before. The next graph shows the results of the answers to the question: Have you previously lived in this community?

Most respondents also had family networks available to them in the place of resettlement. This, as earlier research by DW has shown, provided an important safety net for ex-combatants. Slightly more than one third (33%) of respondents had returned to places where their parents or grandparents were still resident, while 27% were reunited with their siblings, and 21% were reunited with distant relatives.

Furthermore, of those who had chosen to resettle somewhere they had never lived before, over half had chosen to do so because they had family relations there, as can be seen in the next table.

Graph 4: Previous ties to resettlement locations

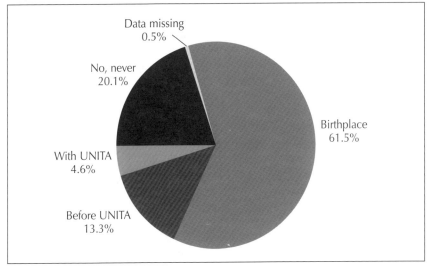

Table 9: Family Ties to Resettlement Locations

Family in resettlement location	Frequency	Percent
Parents or grandparents	201	33.3
Siblings	160	26.5
Extended family	127	21.1
Nobody	106	17.6
Data missing	9	1.5
Total	**603**	**100.0**

Only 8.5% of respondents resettled in a place where they had never lived before and had no relatives. Within this group, 4% (i.e. almost half) were accompanying their spouse, perhaps to his/her birthplace (in fact, almost 80% of the ex-combatants chose places to settle because they were accompanying their spouses, which in most cases was a man accompanying his wife). This leaves a minority of 4.5% who have no apparent ties to the place in which they have resettled – a particularly vulnerable group according to previous research conducted by DW. The motivation for choosing the place of resettlement correlates roughly with previous ties to the community – most chose to return to their birth place or to join family relatives.

Marital status & household structure

As can be seen in the graph below, the vast majority of former combatants have a spouse, although in most cases this is a "common law" rather than a legal marriage. In addition, 16% of respondents claimed to have a second and in some cases a third wife.

While the majority returned/resettled with their immediate family, only 9% returned alone or were unaccompanied. Moreover, 81% were accompanied by their spouses (including 10% who returned with 2 or more wives); 76% brought children with them, and 7% were accompanied by other family relatives.

The overwhelming majority of respondents (93%) identified themselves as 'head of household' – with the average household containing 9 people, although they ranged from 1 to 24. Many former combatants had other

Graph 5: Marital Status of Ex-Combatants

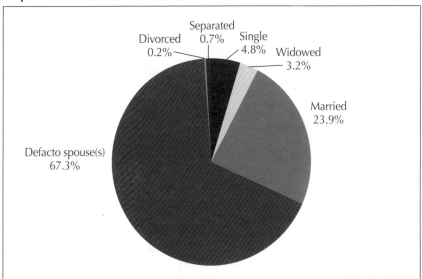

family relatives living with them (extended families): 8% had their parents living with them, 12% were living with adult relatives (aunts, cousins, etc); 14% were supporting child relatives (nieces, nephews etc); and 15% were also supporting orphans within their household.

When compared to the 16% of respondents who claimed to have a second (and in some cases a third wife) it is interesting to note that only 8% counted a second wife as part of their household, implying that some did not consider them part of their direct household but as separate from it. Whether this is a result of the type of nomadic existence experienced during the war, in which former combatants would be stationed in different areas for long periods of time and create families in these areas, or other factors (of a cultural or religious nature) upon their resettlement and return, warrants further research.

Rank and length of military service

The highest rank of those surveyed was Colonel, with very few with the rank of Major or above (25 out of 603). Almost half fell into the lower-middle ranks of Lieutenant to Sergeant, while the lowest ranks (Private and Cadet) accounted for just over a third of respondents.

Table 10: Rank of Former Combatants

Rank	Frequency	Percent
Colonel	4	0.7%
Lieutenant-Colonel	1	0.2%
Major	20	3.3%
Captain	77	12.8%
Lieutenant	130	21.6%
2nd Lieutenant	108	17.9%
Warrant Officer	84	13.9%
Sergeant	46	7.6%
2nd Sergeant	7	1.2%
Private	120	19.9%
Unspecified/other	6	1.0%
Total	**603**	**100.0%**

An interesting finding arose during the project's interim workshop with Angolan stakeholders held in Johannesburg in September 2004. As the results relating to rank were discussed, a number of participants correctly noted that some of the ranks were not typical, or did not exist within UNITA's military structures. The question asked in the survey questionnaire had been: 'What was your rank in the army [FALA]?' to which the respondent could choose from one of the following 10 choices: Colonel, Major, Captain, Lieutenant, Cadet, Sergeant, 2nd Sergeant, Private, and Other. When the results obtained were treated statistically, we found that a number of respondents had given themselves ranks not included in the survey questionnaire. These additional ranks (shown in Table 10 below) included Lieutenant-Colonel and 2nd Lieutenant. In addition, participants at the workshop noted that the rank of 2nd Sergeant (included in the questionnaire) also did not exist in FALA's structures.

Participants at the workshop reflected on the possible meaning(s) and policy implications of these findings. Many thought that the widespread expectation that the higher the rank, the better the benefits accrued by former combatants could explain the artificial inflation of ranks during

Table 11: Rank of Former Combatants (revised)

Rank (new)	Frequency	%
Colonel	4	0.7%
Lieutenant-colonel	1	0.2%
Major	20	3.3%
Captain	77	12.8%
Lieutenant	238	39.5%
Warrant officer	84	13.9%
Sergeant	53	8.8%
Private	120	19.9%
Unspecified/other	6	1.0%
Total	**603**	**100.0%**

the administration of surveys (for example, a Sergeant claiming to be a 2nd Lieutenant). Another possibility was that because the three ranks do in fact exist in the structure of the Angolan Armed Forces (FAA) they might be considered relatively safer, better options by former combatants expecting socio-economic reintegration support, as well as the possibility of future pensions at the level of FAA veterans. Of course, this inconsistency may simply be due to misunderstanding of the questions and the multiple-choice answers.

After some discussion, and following the suggestions and recommendations of Angolan participants (and in particular those directly involved in demobilisation and reintegration activities) a new version of the data was produced. In this new version (see table 11 below) the ranks with discrepancies were collapsed into single ranks: for example, the Lieutenant and 2nd Lieutenant ranks all became Lieutenant, and the Sergeant and 2nd Sergeant were all collapsed into Sergeant.

The number of years an ex-combatant had spent with UNITA was, on average, 17 years, with a range of less than 1 year to 36 years.

The average age at which ex-combatants joined UNITA was 17 years (mean 17.6; median 17.0). We also note that, because the reported age ranged

Graph 6: Time Spent with UNITA

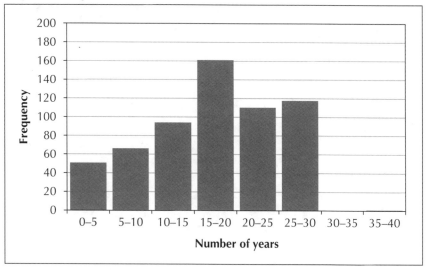

from 3 to 56. This might indicate cases where individual former combatants were abducted and/or brought up within UNITA, rather than the actual age at which they joined the armed forces. The issue of possible abduction and forced recruitment is one that will require considerable attention and future research – adequate treatment of it is naturally outside the specific objectives of this project.

Demobilisation

A first step towards understanding the role and type of intervention strategies that might better support the socio-economic reintegration of ex-combatants is to assess to what extent the former combatant has been officially demobilised. Reinsertion and reintegration support will often only be granted when they have proof of demobilisation.

A considerable majority of respondents (79.4%) confirmed having all their demobilisation documents, and only 8.6% have no documents at all. The results obtained regarding the process of demobilisation are detailed below.

In addition, the project aimed to assess the extent to which former combatants were given demobilisation subsidies or any kind of reinsertion support. These payments are often considered 'transitional safety nets' – as

Table 12: Ex-Combatants in Possession of Demobilisation Documentation

Municipality		Q: Do you have demobilisation documentation?				Total
		Yes, all	Yes, some	No, none	Data missing	
Kuito	Frequency	49	5	1	1	56
	Percent	87.5%	8.9%	1.8%	1.8%	100.0%
Andulo	Frequency	120	19	13	0	152
	Percent	78.9%	12.5%	8.6%	0.0%	100.0%
Huambo Sede	Frequency	70	12	12	1	95
	Percent	73.7%	12.6%	12.6%	1.1%	100.0%
Vila Nova	Frequency	72	16	9	1	98
	Percent	73.5%	16.3%	9.2%	1.0%	100.0%
Lubango	Frequency	60	5	11	0	76
	Percent	78.9%	6.6%	14.5%	0.0%	100.0%
Chipindo	Frequency	108	12	6	0	126
	Percent	85.7%	9.5%	4.8%	0.0%	100.0%
Total	Frequency	479	69	52	3	603
	Percent	79.4%	11.4%	8.6%	0.5%	100.0%

De Watteville has noted: 'the primary purpose of the transitional safety net is to assist the ex-combatant for a certain period – normally between six and twelve months – after demobilisation, and cover his or her basic needs and, preferably, those of the ex-combatants' family'.[97] Only 53.1% of ex-combatants interviewed confirmed they had received the demobilisation subsidy, while 46.6% claim to not have received it. In addition, there were considerable differences between different municipalities, as is evident in the table below, which must be investigated further. More specifically, there seems to be a substantial difference between rural and urban municipalities, with a large percentage of those from urban municipalities (Huambo Sede, Kuíto and Lubango) claiming not to have received demobilisation subsidies.

Table 13: Ex-Combatants who Received the Demobilisation Subsidy

Municipality		Q: Did you receive the demobilisation subsidy?			Total
		yes	no	data missing	
Huambo Sede	Frequency	35	59	1	95
	Percent	36.8%	62.1%	1.1%	100.0%
Vila Nova	Frequency	66	32	0	98
	Percent	67.3%	32.7%	0.0%	100.0%
Kuito	Frequency	24	32	0	56
	Percent	42.9%	57.1%	0.0%	100.0%
Andulo	Frequency	42	109	1	152
	Percent	27.6%	71.7%	0.7%	100.0%
Lubango	Frequency	45	31	0	76
	Percent	59.2%	40.8%	0.0%	100.0%
Chipindo	Frequency	108	18	0	126
	Percent	85.7%	14.3%	0.0%	100.0%
Total	**Frequency**	**320**	**281**	**2**	**603**
	Percent	**53.1%**	**46.6%**	**0.3%**	**100.0%**

In order to assess the level of support for emergency reinsertion at the time of demobilisation, the project asked interviewees whether they had received the demobilisation kit. Only 59.7% of respondents had received it, leaving a substantial proportion of respondents (40%) without this critical component of reinsertion assistance. In fact, several of the focus group interviews confirmed that a substantial number had not benefited from this kind of support, either at the time of demobilisation or when resettled. This was the case with the high ranking officers' group in Andulo, the demobilised focus group in Muembessi commune in Huambo, as well as the low-ranking officers' group in Chipindo. The Chipindo group added that they had had no choice but to survive by collecting firewood and live off WFP supplies.

However, and in sharp contrast to the information gathered through our surveys, data gathered through key interviews presented a different picture. For example, according to the Provincial Secretary of UNITA in Huíla, only 12.2% percent of all former combatants in the province had not received demobilisation kits. The statistics given to the project were as follows:

Table 14: Reinsertion Support: Provision of Demobilisation Kits and Subsidies in Huíla Province

Demobilised who have received kits	Demobilised without kits	Demobilised who have received subsidy	Demobilised who have not received subsidy	Total demobilised in the Province
6,925	967	4,128	3,764	**7,892**

In Andulo, the deputy administrator (a former UNITA officer) pointed out to the team that although former combatants were given 'household' kits and contingency subsidies, many of them had sold them and spent the money on articles with no real economic value.

In any case, because the project conducted its surveys in Andulo during a distribution of agricultural kits, the overall impression was that many former combatants were receiving agricultural kits for the first time. In Huambo (Muembessi commune), a focus group discussion with demobilised soldiers confirmed that they too were still waiting for assistance promised in the form of agricultural kits, and that only CARE had provided them with some seeds and tools.

CHAPTER 3

THE ECONOMIC, SOCIAL AND POLITICAL DIMENSIONS OF REINTEGRATION
Findings

Economic dimensions of reintegration

Economic reintegration contributes to financial independence and self-reliance which is viewed as essential for achieving objectives of demobilisation at the social and political level.[98]

The last step of a DRP (demobilisation and reintegration programme) is a long-term process that starts at the same time as reinsertion and focuses on the reintegration of ex-combatants and families. A successful reintegration is completed when ex-combatants and families are able to generate enough income to ensure their financial independence and when the community has accepted them.[99]

Household income and economic security

In order to assess former combatants' socio-economic situation, and to obtain some understanding of the level of economic security of the former combatant's household, the project included a considerable number of questions focusing on issues such as the number of people that contribute to the household's income; the former combatant's main and secondary economic activities; questions on house ownership and access to land, and so on.

The project found that, in over half the cases (54%), the former combatant's household has two income earners – the ex-combatant and his spouse. An additional 30% of the respondents indicated that more than two people were responsible for the household's livelihood – implying that in only 16% of cases is the ex-combatant solely responsible for household income and economic security. Most former combatants (76%) have some secondary source of income, and some even a tertiary. Notably, over half of these are receiving aid from the WFP or another NGO. In the graph below, 'unearned' includes NGO and WFP handouts, as well as support

Graph 7: Sources of Income

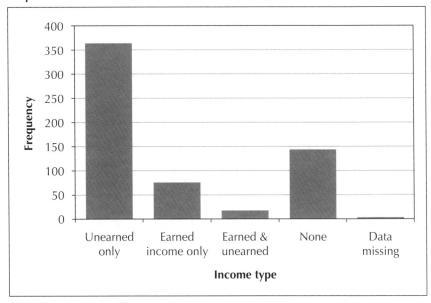

Graph 8: Sources of Food for Returned and Resident Groups[100]

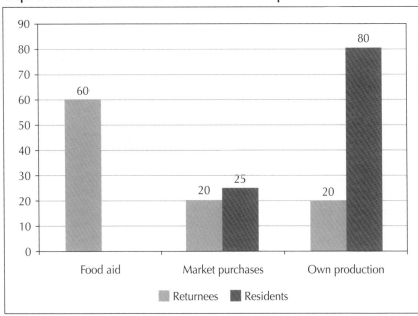

from family/friends, while 'earned' includes income from wage labour and trade.

The dependence on emergency assistance from the WFP and other NGOs was pointed out in several of the focus group discussions and key informant interviews. This was the situation in Chipindo for a group of low-ranking officers, for the group of demobilised soldiers in Andulo, as well as for the group of community leaders in Bairro Santos. Interviews with WFP in Kuíto confirmed that the agency's resettlement support had been centred on food assistance during the first two years after the Luena MoU? for all population groups (since demobilisation, including former combatants) as well as support to local administrations for the rehabilitation and reconstruction of infrastructure.

Data generated by the inter-agency group tasked with monitoring vulnerability in Bié province for the same period[101] shows that, although the overall dependency on food aid diminished after the Luena MoU, it still represented the single most important source of food for people who had resettled and/or returned. Perhaps more important is the fact that returned communities had begun producing their own food, albeit of insufficient quantity. The graph below, produced by the inter-agency

Graph 9: House Ownership

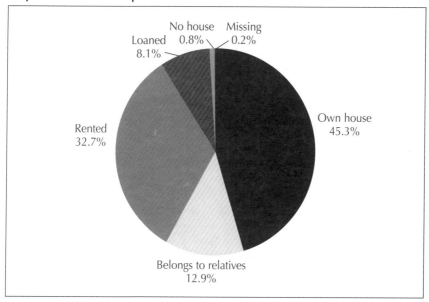

Graph 10: Access to and Ownership of Land

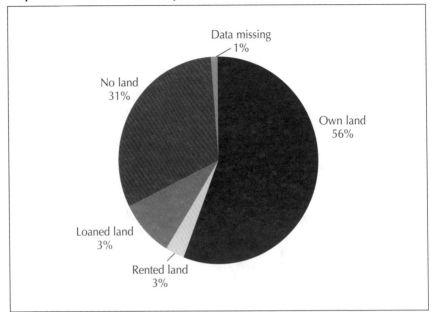

group shows the relative weight of food aid (*ajuda alimentar*), market purchases (*aquisições de mercado*) and own production (*produção própria*) for both the resettled/returned group (*retornados*) as well as residents (*residentes*):

As regards house ownership, just fewer than half the former combatants surveyed (45.3%) claimed to own the house in which they were living. Additional research would be required to determine whether this high level of house ownership was a result, for example, of inheritance and/or allocation by the community (since the majority chose to resettle in the place in which they were born) or of purchase (unlikely because most former combatants did not have the necessary capital).

As to the remainder, one third of interviewees rented; 8% had been loaned a house, and 13% lived in a house belonging to relatives. An extreme group of just under 1% claimed themselves as 'homeless'.

A similar situation was found in terms of access to and ownership of land, as can be seen in the next graph. Compared to the 45.3% claiming to own their own house, 56% claimed to own land. Some 9% of interviewees had been loaned land (8% had been loaned a house), and a further 3% were renting (in this case, the discrepancy is wider). However, a substantial percentage – approximately 31% – did not own, rent or had been loaned land.

Primary economic activity

Somewhat expectedly, the project found that the principal sources of ex-combatants' livelihoods varied dramatically between rural and urban areas – though the urban/rural distinction is not always clear-cut. Although over half the sample (55%) cited agriculture as the principal source of income, the figure was 71% in rural areas but just 28% in urban areas.

The next most common source of livelihoods was wage labour, at 21%. Once again, the urban/rural' differences were considerable: while 39% claimed wage labour as their primary source of income in urban areas, this percentage fell to 11% in rural municipalities. Informal trade and commerce was the principal source of livelihood for a combined total of 13% (19% urban, 10% rural). It is worth noting that only 0.3% of respondents were

Graph 11: Principal sources of livelihoods: Urban areas

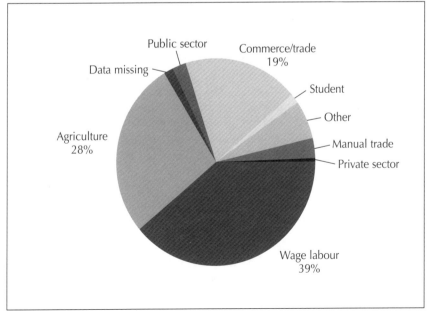

Graph 12: Principal sources of livelihoods: Rural areas

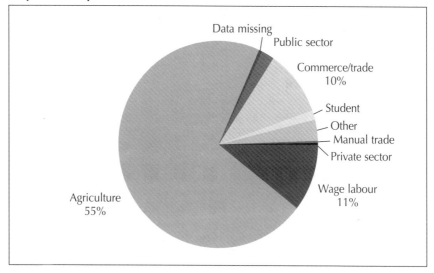

formally employed in the private sector – an issue to which we will return later.

Previous Occupation and Training

A very important component of this project – and one that should play a fundamental role in the design of reintegration programmes – was to determine the set of professional skills existing within the sample surveyed. To this end, the survey questionnaire included three distinct questions: (1) What was your occupation before joining the armed movement? (2) Did you receive any professional training before joining? and (3) Did you receive any professional training during your time with UNITA? (Appendix 1 shows the full set of questions and possible answers).

The project found that, prior to joining UNITA, almost half were small-scale farmers. Significantly, perhaps reflecting the relatively young age at which many joined UNITA's armed forces, just over a third of the group were still studying. In addition, a higher proportion than currently were employed (both in the public and private sectors) or otherwise working in manual trades. The general range of occupations registered was higher (5% had been tradesmen versus just 1% now, and 6% had worked in the public sector, primarily as teachers or nurses, versus 2% now).

Table 15: Did you receive any professional training during your time with UNITA?

Sector of training	Frequency	% of cases
Skilled manual trade	103	17.1
Public sector (nurse, teacher)	90	14.9
Administration/finance	9	1.5
Agriculture	6	1.0
Political/social mobilisation	6	1.0
None	404	67.0
Other	9	1.5

The majority (80%) had no training at all before joining UNITA. Of those with some training, most (13% of the total) were in a broad range of manual trades (plumbers, carpenters, electricians, etc), and the remainder (6%) in public sector professions (nurses, teachers, etc)., a third of interviewees said they had received some form of professional training while with UNITA – in most cases they were trained in a manual trade, teaching or nursing.

We should note that the issue of the incorporation of UNITA teachers and nurses into the public service was raised in several of the focus-group sessions. Former combatants pointed out that this had been promised at the time of demobilisation, echoing a national debate on the issue of equivalence of training between public sector workers and their own cadres. The group of high-ranking officers in Andulo, for example, commented that although they had supplied a list of all former combatants with formal qualifications for integration into the civil service, only a third of them had in fact been incorporated. Focus groups in Huambo also suggested that, in addition to the relevant documentation, it was necessary to have contacts (normally family, occasionally friends) and/or money in order to be employed in the civil service.

Social Dimensions of Reintegration

Own Perspectives on Reintegration

A key project aim was to deepen our understanding of the relationship between identity and reintegration. In particular, the project planned a

Table 16: Ex-Combatants' Own Perceptions of Reintegration

Reintegrated into civilian life?	Frequency	Percent
Yes	463	76.8
No	137	22.7
Data missing	3	0.5
Total	**603**	**100.0**

participatory assessment of former combatants' own perceptions of whether they saw still themselves (two years after the end of the war) as soldiers, as demobilised soldiers, or as civilians. A series of questions was devised to assess former combatants' own perceptions of whether they considered themselves to be reintegrated into civilian life and if not, what would make this possible.

The majority of respondents (77%) considered themselves to be reintegrated into civilian life, as evident in the table below.

A smaller proportion of respondents (just over half) saw themselves as civilians, however, with almost an equal number seeing themselves as

Graph 13: Ex-Combatants' Own Identity Perception

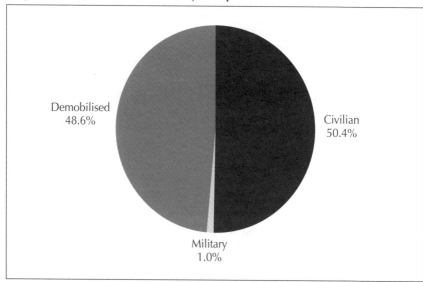

Demobilised 48.6%

Civilian 50.4%

Military 1.0%

'demobilised'. A very small number still saw themselves as 'military', however, and a similarly small number (2.3%) said they had considered a return to military life since their demobilisation. It appears that while ex-combatants no longer saw themselves as combatants or military personnel, for many there was still some way to go before the transition to civilian life was complete. Some 22.7% (a considerable number of respondents) did not consider themselves reintegrated into civilian life.

The focus groups helped shed additional light on this issue. Some mentioned that the 'demobilised' identity was useful because it enabled them to access aid and assistance from WFP, NGOs and the government. This has a downside as well though – some ex-combatants went as far as to say that, while they would very much like to be seen as civilians, it is made rather difficult by all these NGOs (and researchers presumably!) who keep turning up and asking to speak to 'the demobilised'.

Social networks and community participation

The survey attempted to gauge ex-combatants' participation in the fabric of community social and organisational life. The most common form of social activity and network appears to be linked to the churches, with almost two thirds of ex-combatants (64%) being members of a church. In almost all cases, they had attended the same church before joining UNITA, and one which existed in their place of resettlement.

Perhaps surprisingly, given much of what has been written about UNITA and the central highlands region, the group surveyed contained more Catholics than Protestants. However, it is probable that the Catholic church did, in fact, attract more followers – a survey done in 1960 showed that 69% of Huambo's population were Catholics and 27% Protestant, while in Bié the equivalent figures were 44% and 30%, respectively. Both of these are higher than the national average of 17% Protestants, however, and the popular myth of a close association between UNITA and the Protestant church may perhaps simply reflect the fact that, in the early days of UNITA activity, Jonas Savimbi used the Methodist missionary network as a vehicle to gain popular support in the central highlands.

In most cases, but not all, former combatants' self-professed religion corresponded with the church of which they were a member. A small minority claimed to be, for instance, Catholic but were members of a Protestant church.

Graph 14: Organisational membership

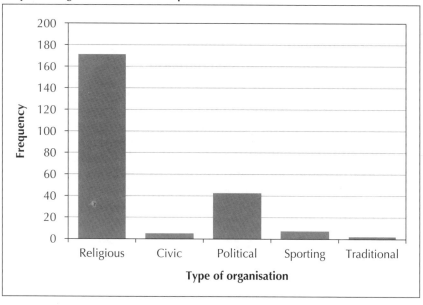

It is significant that a majority of respondents (63%) reported that they were not a member of any organisation as such. Of those who were, the organisations were most commonly linked to the churches – e.g. choirs, women's groups, men's groups. 'Political organisations' most frequently referred to LIMA (UNITA women's' group), JURA (UNITA youth group) or to UNITA party membership.

Around half of those who were members of an organisation held some kind of position of responsibility within that organisation, i.e. 15% of the total of ex-combatants. Although a high number of these positions were within political organisations (24 of 93), in fact, the highest number (62 of 93) were in religious organisations. This would seem to indicate a relatively high level of reintegration and social acceptance among this group, because they had been able, in a short period of time, to not only access social networks but to also make some kind of progress up the organisational hierarchy.

This does assume, however, that these are not networks that the ex-combatants brought with them, which could imply, for instance, the establishment of new churches and associations. This seems unlikely because the vast majority of ex-combatants reported that they were not members of a church while with UNITA. This is unsurprising given the degree of social and political control maintained over the organisation by its leadership and, in particular, by Jonas Savimbi. Yet researchers did report seeing some new churches in Bié province, which could have been built since the resettlement process – but more likely to be linked simply to the influx of money from missionary associations of various denominations since the end of the war. This will be an interesting topic for further research, however, because even though societal networks and associations have been in a clear state of flux since the end of the war, it is not yet clear how or what the implications of that may be.

Interpersonal links and support networks

Beyond 'formal' membership of organisations, an additional dimension of reintegration refers to informal social interactions and networks. The project attempted to gain some insight into the informal social networks to which ex-combatants have access in two ways: by including four questions in the survey questionnaire, and by focusing on interpersonal links and support networks in the focus group discussions. Survey questions included: (1) *With whom do you spend most of your time?* (2) *To whom do you turn to in times of need?* and, (3) *Who, in your opinion, is the most important person in your community?*

The graph below shows that while the family is the most important source of social interaction for ex-combatants (442 respondents), they also interact with each other (178 respondents). The church is also an important locus of social networking, although it is unclear whether this is a cause or a result of the high level of church membership.

A further dimension the project explored was the nature and extent of the support networks to which ex-combatants had access and, in particular, the people they could/would turn to in case of problems. It is generally assumed that the *Soba* is the person to whom communities turn when problems arise, the one who will resolve conflicts, allocate land or shelter when needed, arrange support for the sick, the old and the disabled, and so on. Indeed, the results seem to show that the *Soba* is the entity most commonly chosen, but even so, this accounts for less than half of cases (293 respondents). As can be seen in the graph below, almost one third said they would go to their family or spouse, and one in 10 to their church.

These findings may help elucidate the present status of traditional authorities in a limited number of municipalities and for a specific

Graph 15: Social Interaction

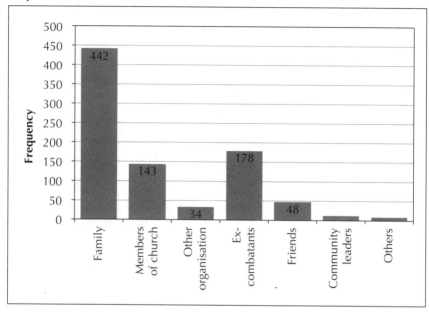

Graph 16: Problem-Solving Within the Community

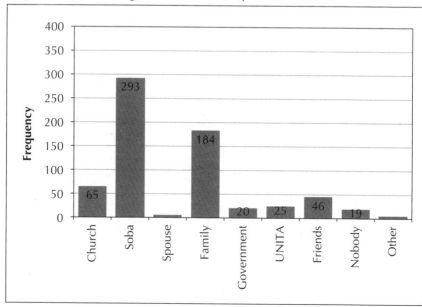

caseload, that of former combatants. However, after decades of civil war, displacement and the erosion of the traditional social fabric at local level, this is an issue that demands further empirical research. Many *Sobas* in the area of our fieldwork had returned to their communities only in 2002 or 2003, and so were as much a part of the process of resettlement and reintegration as the displaced and demobilised people they were supposed to 'oversee'.[102]

Significantly, few respondents (less than 5%) said they would turn to UNITA in case of problems – and an equal number would go to the government. Even fewer (3%) said they would have nobody to turn to. This represents a major shift for ex-combatants – whilst with UNITA almost all said that they would turn to a military superior or member of the political committee within UNITA (closely interlinked and indistinguishable in some cases).

Perceptions of Authority

The survey also attempted to gauge ex-combatants' relations with communities, and their perception of authority and hierarchy outside of the military structures of UNITA. While the question above (who would you turn to in case of problems) gives some indication of this, the project asked an additional question: *Who do you consider to be the most important person in the community?*

Despite the fact that only slightly less than half of the respondents claimed that they would go to the *Soba* in case of problems, it appears that traditional authorities retain a strong symbolic importance in the minds of ex-combatants. The vast majority of respondents considered the *Soba* to be the most important person in the community – as can be seen in the table above. This was echoed in focus group discussions – the *Soba* was still regarded as a central figure by almost everyone. Nevertheless, while their symbolic authority was still respected, participants in focus group discussions recognised that the *Sobas'* actual powers were, in practice, becoming more and more limited.

The issue of trust may be paramount in this context. The *Soba* and church leaders, for example, are perceived to be more important than both the local state representative (the administrator) and the more openly politicised figures such as an MPLA or UNITA party representative. This may be evidence of a higher degree of trust in both *Sobas* and church leaders because local level government (in the form of the local administrator) is normally either an

Graph 17: Ex-Combatants' perceptions of authority in the community

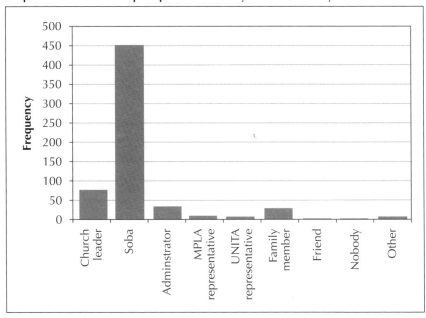

MPLA member or at least an appointee of the government. The local context and knowledge of individual leaders by ex-combatants almost certainly plays an additional role in determining the levels of trust and perceived authority of the different kinds of leaders.

Community response to ex-combatants

In the immediate aftermath of the war, a critical concern of humanitarian agencies as well as some government departments was that the simultaneous movement (organised and spontaneous) of return and resettlement of the different affected groups could increase the level of conflict at local level. The fact that several thousand former combatants as well as hundreds of thousands of displaced people 'descended' with little or no support at the village level was viewed with some apprehension.[103] How these different groups would relate to one another, and especially to those who stayed behind (residents), in a context of severe scarcity of resources was a question to which few had convincing answers. In addition, and because former combatants were (to a certain extent) being targeted differently to other vulnerable groups, the prospect of rising friction at community level between civilians and recently demobilised soldiers was a working hypothesis for many involved in the resettlement and return process.

As noted at the outset, this project aimed to understand whether, and to what extent, programmes that target ex-combatants differently from other vulnerable groups actually inhibit reintegration. The programmes might be reinforcing the sense of difference experienced by ex-combatants as well as the cleavages that might separate them from the communities that now received them. Assuming that successful reintegration is predicated on the positive *transformation* of modalities of behaviour and, more importantly, identities formed under conditions of conflict, we asked the following question: could special treatment aimed at ex-combatants actually inhibit or delay reintegration?

As a first step towards answering this question, the project started by looking at the way in which communities received former combatants. Former combatants were asked the following questions: (1) *Do you consider yourself to have been well received by the community?* and (2) *What did the community do to receive (welcome) you?* The answers obtained go some way toward explaining the type of relationship between former combatants and the communities living in areas of resettlement, but we should point out that the findings might be specific to the central highlands.

Box 2: Traditional Ceremonies and Reintegration

The project sought to examine (in limited fashion) this aspect of the reintegration process to assess to what extent this dimension featured in the expectations and experience of ex-soldiers. Interestingly, none of the respondents brought up traditional ceremonies in the context of the project's general surveying on attitudes, either individually or within focus groups. However, when specifically probed via follow-on focus group work, all respondents acknowledged that not only had traditional ceremonies been important in the past as markers of change and social acceptance, but that ceremonies were, in many cases, expected by ex-soldiers and their families upon their return to civilian life. As one spouse of a former combatant said, *'traditional ceremonies are synonymous with happiness, satisfaction, they lift morale of those that return, push away malign spirits and help everyone to forget sad events witnessed in the past: all this helps reintegration'*. However, few of the respondents indicated that they had indeed experienced traditional welcoming and healing ceremonies. They ascribed this to a number of factors: the lack of financial resources needed to conduct the ceremonies amongst families and communities welcoming former combatants; the death or displacement of the elders who knew the traditions; and the fact some ex-combatants had settled in areas that were not their places of origin.

Graph 18: Community reception of ex-combatants (I)

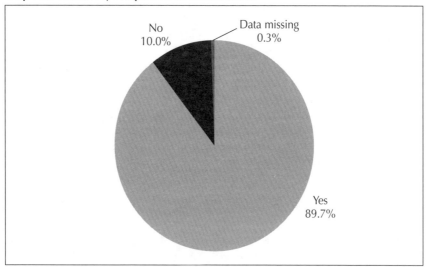

The majority of ex-combatants (90%) said they were well received by the communities in which they resettled, although there is no clear definition of what is meant by this. In most cases it seemed to imply allocation of land and housing, donation of material goods such as clothes, utensils or food, or the holding of some kind of meeting or party. Brief descriptions of these were given (food, alcohol, dancing) but none specifically mentioned any kind of formal welcome or traditional ceremony – although a traditional demobilisation and purification ceremony for people who have killed someone does exist in the central highlands. It might simply not have been discussed, or it might not have taken place. In any case, the fact that most respondents did not mention any kind of formal reception on arrival is surprising given the normal level of formality in Angolan society, and invites further research.

Of the 10% who said that they were not well received, the most common complaints were social – in the form of verbal abuse or social discrimination. A smaller number complained of lack of allocation of land, housing or other items.

Overall, just under half said that they had been allocated land and/or housing – although this level is lower than had been assumed, it may reflect a strong link to house ownership (as previously noted standing at 45.3%) as well as land ownership (at 56%). Almost one third received food and/or

Graph 19: Community reception of ex-combatants (II)

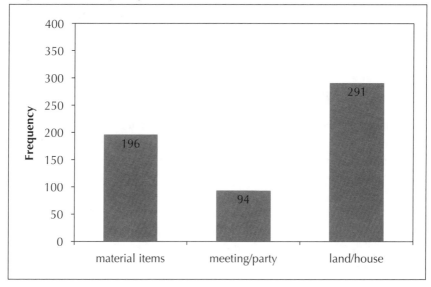

other material goods (e.g. clothes, money, kitchen utensils) and around one sixth were welcomed with a party or community meeting.

Around 13% said they were neither welcomed nor given anything on arrival. This is just slightly higher than the number who specified that they were 'not well received' and represents more or less the same group of people.

Political dimensions of reintegration

The political dimensions of reintegration are often forgotten (or deliberately left aside) in the implementation of reintegration programmes. Furthermore, and with few exceptions, hardly any studies have paid attention to these critical elements of reintegration.[104] At the outset of this monograph, we noted that beyond a commitment to demilitarisation and an end to the use of violent means in the resolution of disputes, a deeper commitment by all at a social-political level is needed if post-war societies are to sustain the peace. This presupposes that the peaceful and active participation of former combatants in the political process of their societies must be regarded as a critical component of peace-building, and that successful reintegration depends not only on social acceptance and economic self-reliance but also on political participation. Moreover, and as noted by Kingma, 'in the longer term the reintegration (also) depends on the process of democratisation, including the recovery of a weak (or collapsed) state and the maturing of an independent civil society'.[105]

As discussed in the introduction, 27 years of protracted civil war in Angola came to an end with the signature of the Luena 'Memorandum of Understanding'. In fact, the commitments undertaken by both belligerents at the Angolan National Assembly on 4 April 2002, in particular to resume the stalled Lusaka peace process, reflected a real change in circumstances prevailing in the country. Having experienced the consequences of two failed peace processes with catastrophic consequences, the belief in genuine political reconciliation between the former adversaries had up to that point appeared more and more elusive.[106]

At the time the fieldwork part of the project began (January 2004) the government announced that legislative elections would be held at the end of 2006, following which presidential elections would be held (in 2007 at best). Up to that point, both the government and UNITA had demonstrated a strong public commitment to peace and reconciliation, and the successful observation of the quartering, disarmament and demobilisation process was often given as definitive proof that reconciliation was not at stake. To be sure, there was some level of disagreement within the Joint Military Commission (JMC) as regards the DD&R process, and in particular its reintegration phase – however, these disagreements did not halt the process.

Although highly situation- and actor-specific, combatants are often recruited on the basis of some kind of political project, and during their time with an armed movement they may experience constant mobilisation on the basis of the goals of such project. Although more research needs to be undertaken as regards the mobilisation tactics used in UNITA, the words of General Paulo Lukamba 'Gato' while president of the movement's Management Committee in the immediate aftermath of the war hint at what he saw as the core 'political nature' of all UNITA soldiers. When asked how he foresaw the transformation of UNITA from a military to a political movement he retorted: 'we have always been a political movement. All of us joined UNITA first and foremost because we agreed with its political project. We became military people later'.[107]

In order to gauge the extent to which former combatants were aware and interested in the political process, the project devised a series of questions that were included in the survey questionnaire. We asked former combatants: (1) *Have you heard about the next elections?* (2) *If so, from whom?* (3) *Do you know of any political parties?* (4) *In your opinion, to vote is...* (5) *Do you think elections are important to consolidate peace?* (6) *Did you vote in the 1992 elections?* (7) *Will you vote in the next elections?* (8) *Will you participate in the election campaign?* (9) *If so, how?*

Elections and voting

When asked about whether they were aware of the next elections, the overwhelming majority of respondents (96%) responded positively. As can be seen in the table below, nearly all respondents considered elections important to the consolidation of peace in the country. This was echoed by focus group discussions, as well as by the more qualitative responses in the survey.

Most former combatants speak of elections as 'allowing for the choice of a government that can attend to its people's needs'. A minority of individuals in the survey, and several of the higher/middle ranking officers' focus groups, specifically mentioned the need for a change in regime and the need for a new leader – and there were several references to the fact that the 1992 elections were 'stolen' from UNITA. Interestingly, even very young ex-combatants referred to the 1992 elections in great detail, as if they had participated in them, indicating the importance they have assumed in popular memory. Community members interviewed in focus groups also viewed elections as important, but were a little more hesitant, more often citing the experience of 1992.

Table 17: Ex-Combatants' perceptions of elections

Are elections are important to consolidate peace?	Frequency	Percent
Yes	585	97.0%
No	11	1.8%
Don't know	1	0.2%
Data missing	6	1.0%
Total	**603**	**100.0%**

Table 18: Ex-Combatants' and the 1992 Elections

Did you vote in the 1992 elections?	Frequency	Percent
Yes	422	70.0%
No	174	28.9%
Data missing	7	1.2%
Total	**603**	**100.0%**

Nearly three quarters of the respondents said that they voted in the 1992 elections. This reflects the fact that recruitment patterns after the outbreak of civil war favoured the youth and approximately a quarter of the respondents were below 18 years of age at the time of the 1992 elections.

There was a near universal positive response on the part of those interviewed to the question as to whether they would vote in the next elections.

It is worthwhile comparing the results above, even if in a careful manner (due to differences in sample size, provinces targeted as well as profile of interviewees), with a survey on attitudes towards elections in Angola conducted on behalf of the International Republican Institute (IRI) during March and April 2003. The survey by IRI found that 72.9% of respondents in the six provinces surveyed outside Luanda (two of which correspond with our own: Huíla and Huambo) planned to vote in the next elections. If one includes Luanda, 68% of respondents to the IRI survey said they planned to vote in the next elections as can be seen below:

Table 19: Ex-Combatants and the Next Elections

Will you vote in the next elections?	Frequency	Percent
Yes	589	97.7%
No	4	0.7%
Data missing	2	0.3%
Don't know	8	1.3%
Total	**603**	**100.0%**

Graph 20: Will you vote in the next elections?

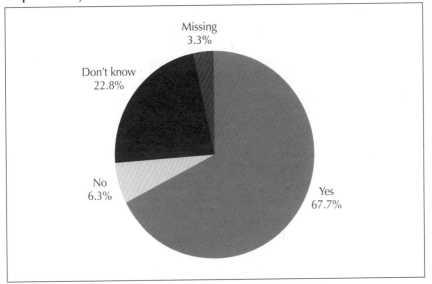

(Survey by IRI during March/April 2003)[108]

Graph 21: In your opinion, voting is....?

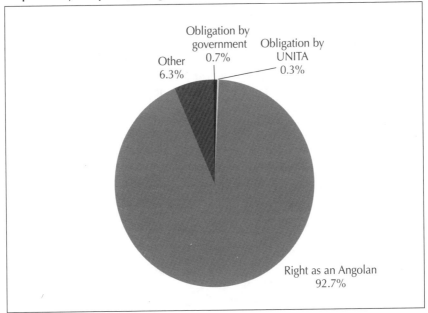

In our survey, 97.7% of former combatants claimed they planned to vote in the next elections. This result is evidence of their strong intention to exercise their right to vote – prefacing perhaps what the Praxis Group has termed the 'point of no return': 'when combatants are asked to give up their arms, they face a point of 'no return': they, and their leaders must have faith in a future where the advantages of peace outweigh those of war'.[109]

A particularly strong response was elicited when ex-soldiers were asked how they would characterise voting, that is, in terms of 'an obligation' owed to the government or UNITA, or as a citizenship right. In fact, more than 90% felt voting was a right. In addition, several focus groups made reference to the fact that they felt freer and more able to vote as citizens now because they were no longer under UNITA supervision, as they had effectively been in 1992.

Knowledge of Political Parties

Over 90% of the respondents knew about Angolan political parties and were able to identify the MPLA and UNITA. Other political parties (some of which were voted into Parliament in the 1992 elections such as the FpD, the PRS or PDP-ANA) were not well known by former combatants. This may be a consequence of the fact that, although the official electoral law allowing for multi-party competition was passed in 1991, resulting in a proliferation of political parties, the reversion to conflict after the 1992 elections brought with it *de facto* restrictions on political party activism across the country. These restrictions have only began to recede once the war ended. Nonetheless, respondents were able to name a number of other parties, though these did not exceed 2.2% of the total.

The group who could only name the MPLA and UNITA was four times bigger than those who could name the MPLA, UNITA and the smaller, more

Table 20: Ex-Combatants' Knowledge of Political Parties (I)

Do you know any political parties?	Frequency	Percent
Yes	550	91.2%
No	50	8.3%
Data missing	3	0.5%
Total	**603**	**100.0%**

Table 21: Ex-Combatants' Knowledge of Political Parties (II)

Do you know any political parties? Which parties?	Frequency	Percent
MPLA and UNITA only	427	70.8%
'New' parties only	13	2.2%
MPLA, UNITA & 'new' parties	107	17.7%
None	53	8.8%
Data missing	3	0.5%
Total	**603**	**100.0%**

recent parties (PRS, FpD, PDP-ANA etc). A minority indicated that they only knew of the newer parties – or perhaps that they saw only these as political parties and not military in some way.

Political Participation and Party Activism

There is a notable split amongst respondents with respect to political activism. For example, slightly more than half (54.1%) indicated that they would be interested in taking part in an election campaign while 46% say they would not. It is worth underscoring that this is a particularly high level of interest in actively participating in politics in a post-conflict state. It might also help clarify the political mobilisation which former combatants experienced while serving in UNITA, as mentioned earlier.

When asked how they would like to participate in electoral events, one fifth of the respondents said they would be interested in participating as candidates in a future election. An equivalent number said that they would be interested in organising events (18.4%) and participating in events (21.4%).

When contrasted with the findings of the IRI survey referred to above, a number of common elements are evident (as before, such a comparison must be done carefully due to differences in sample size, provinces targeted, and the profile of interviewees). In the IRI survey, respondents were surveyed for both 'passive political participation' (essentially focusing on intentions to vote) as well as 'active political participation' (which included membership

Table 22: Participation in Electoral Events

How would you participate in electoral events?	Frequency	Percent of ex-combatants
As a candidate	131	21.7%
By organising events	111	18.4%
By participating events	129	21.4%
Another way	14	2.3%

* Question was asked to respondents who replied 'yes' to 'would you be interested in participating in an electoral campaign and in some cases more than one response was given. Percentages are of the total number of respondents.

of political parties, availability to work in an election campaign, and, finally willingness to stand as candidates).

Interestingly, for our purposes here, were the findings which correlated political party membership and willingness to work in an election campaign and to stand as a candidate. The IRI survey found that political party membership is positively correlated with an individual's availability to work as a political activist: 64.3% of those who are members of a political party are available for this type of work. This result (within those that are active

Graph 22: Ex-Combatants Participation in an Electoral Campaign

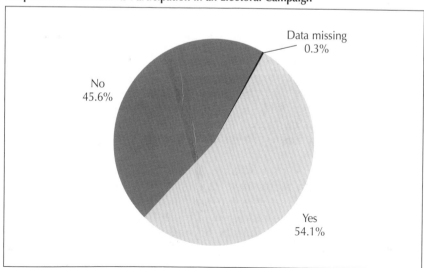

members of political parties) is remarkably similar to the one obtained in our survey (54.1%) – even though one could not presume that all former combatants surveyed remained members or sympathisers of UNITA.[110]

Information Sources

The source of information that predominates is the radio, with 83.4% of respondents using that as their key source – not dissimilar to the majority of Angolans who live outside Luanda and for whom the radio remains a primary (at times the sole) source of information. We should note that access to information (television, radio and print media) is largely limited to Luanda (and to an extent, Benguela and Lubango). Interestingly, the *Soba* appears in second place at 12.4%. Here too, the issue of trust may be a factor that strengthens the importance of traditional leaders as sources of information for their community. Other possible sources of information included UNITA (party) at 6.8%; while the government (government institutions), the MPLA (party) and newspapers received fewer than 5% of responses.

An important distinction with respect to radio is which station is being listened to as a source of information. According to respondents, Angolan state radio is most listened to (33%), while international radio stations and Angolan independent radio stations have markedly lower listenership levels, at 17.2% and 8.5%, respectively. However, the figures on independent Angolan radio stations must be taken with some care because, at the time of the research, no independent Angolan radio

Table 23: Ex-Combatants' Sources of Information: Radio

Which radio stations do you listen to?	Frequency	Percent
Angolan state radio only	200	33.2%
Independent Angolan radio stations	51	8.5%
International but no independent Angolan stations	104	17.2%
Both international and independent Angolan stations	46	7.6%
No access to radio/does not listen	100	16.6%
Data missing	102	16.9%
Total	**603**	**100.0%**

station transmitted nationwide. The well-known case of Radio Ecclésia's efforts to expand its coverage to the whole territory is a paradigmatic example here.

Note that the low level of newspaper readership (under 3%) is due to the fact that there was no regular circulation of newspapers outside the capital at the time – making an equivalent analysis moot.

CHAPTER 4

SURVEYING FOR TRENDS
Correlation of Findings

Surveying for an urban/rural divide

One the assumptions that guided the project's approach was that, within the specific context of post-war Angola, there might be a noticeable difference between those respondents based in urban areas and those based in rural areas. This was reflected in the methodology employed, that is to say, explicitly conducting surveys in both urban and rural areas – even if, as noted at the outset, the distinction between urban and rural is not clear cut. Nevertheless, underlying the approach taken were, first and foremost, assumptions regarding differing economic circumstances found in each area – in particular that in more urbanised areas former combatants might have wider and better possibilities of finding employment in the formal and informal economies, while perhaps experiencing challenges of a different nature (such as on a social and political level). To what extent would the socialising effects of urban life on rural populations be observed in former combatants and what implications – if at all – might these have for their successful reintegration?

Indeed, the sense of the importance of the urban/rural distinction was something that came out in some of the focus group interviews:

> The awareness of people who live in rural and urban (city) environments is very different. Urban people are more informed and advanced, while rural people have no access to information. (Focus Group, Lubango)

A classic (while context insensitive) reading of the process might see rural, tradition-bound villagers moving to the relatively atomized, anonymous and socially less prescriptive environment of the town or city, and being absorbed into that very environment. In fact, what happened under the conditions of rapid, forced migration to urban areas during the many decades of war was quite the contrary: urban life became 'ruralised' in certain respects. Rural social structures were replicated to the extent that they could be in urban and peri-urban settings, and all this happened in the face of the breakdown of centralising institutions and physical infrastructure. This was particularly observed in Lubango, which as noted above, was for many years a relatively safe haven for waves of internal migration.

Perhaps because of the specific provinces chosen, the survey (with a few exceptions) did not find significant differences between rural and urban-based respondents with respect to the many questions involving reintegration. The fact that an urban/rural divide was less meaningful than it otherwise might have been may partly be attributed to the fluidity of population movements (significant rural to urban or peri-urban migration being a common experience in the central plateau region), as well as to very similar levels of vulnerability and employment opportunities.

Nevertheless, because distinctions between what constitutes rural and urban may have introduced some distortions into the data collected, urban/rural trends identified in the data analysis were checked for variations by municipality. Significant variations resulting from this secondary analysis are discussed below – where they are not mentioned it can be assumed that they did not appear, and to the best of our knowledge, the relationship holds.

Firstly, reintegration as perceived by the ex-combatants did vary slightly depending upon whether the respondent was based in a rural (79.5%) or urban (72.2%) area. When asked if they considered themselves to be reintegrated, or saw themselves as civilian, demobilised or military, a remarkably similar response was elicited from rural and urban participants in the survey:

However, when the data is broken down by municipality and province, a different picture appears – in both Bié province (Andulo and Kuíto) and

Table 24: Perceptions of Reintegration in Rural and Urban Areas

Reintegrated in civilian life?	Urban or rural					
	Rural		Urban		Total	
	Frequency	Percent	Frequency	Percent	Frequency	Percent
Yes	299	79.9%	164	72.6%	463	77.2%
No	75	20.1%	62	27.4%	137	22.8%
Total	374	100.0%	226	100.0%	600	100.0%

Table 25: Perceptions of Identity by Municipality

Municipality		Do you consider yourself...			Total
		Civilian	Military	Demobilised	
Kuito	Frequency	30	2	24	**56**
	Percent	53.6%	3.6%	42.9%	**100.0%**
Andulo	Frequency	60	3	89	**152**
	Percent	39.5%	2.0%	58.6%	**100.0%**
Lubango	Frequency	27	.0	49	**76**
	Percent	35.5%	.0	64.5%	**100.0%**
Chipindo	Frequency	74	.0	52	**126**
	Percent	58.7%	.0	41.3%	**100.0%**
Huambo Sede	Frequency	59	.0	36	**95**
	Percent	62.1%	.0	37.9%	**100.0%**
Vila Nova	Frequency	54	1	43	**98**
	Percent	55.1%	1.0%	43.9%	**100.0%**
Total	**Frequency**	**304**	**6**	**293**	**603**
	Percent	**50.4%**	**1.0%**	**48.6%**	**100.0%**

Huambo province (Huambo Sede and Vila Nova), ex-combatants in urban areas were more likely to view themselves as civilians. In Huíla (Lubango and Chipindo), the relationship is reversed, and those in urban areas were considerably less likely to view themselves as civilians. This is interesting because Lubango is, by generally accepted standards of urban life, the only real city in this data sample.[111]

In Andulo, former combatants exhibited a relatively lower propensity to view themselves as 'civilians' (39.5% of respondents versus, for example, 62.1% in Huambo). One could infer that the Andulo response might have been obtained because, at the time of the survey, former combatants had received WFP food assistance and (for the first time since the end of the war) seeds and tools. They would not have wanted their status as 'former combatants' questioned at that precise moment in time. However, a similar situation was encountered in Vila Nova (Huambo), where the proportion of those who regarded themselves as 'civilians' was considerably higher. One possible explanation may instead be associated with the generally high levels of political activism exhibited by ex-combatants in Andulo. Focus groups done in Andulo show a higher level of political awareness and a stronger degree of association with UNITA than seen elsewhere.

> ...the term demobilised or ex-combatant will take time to disappear because even though he is no longer involved in military activity, he has military attitudes and reservations that result from the time spent in the military forces [sic]. Furthermore, civilians within communities use this term [demobilised] to be able to more easily identify within the community someone who belonged to UNITA in the past. *(Focus Group, middle-ranking officers, Andulo, translation by the authors).*

The reception experienced by the ex-combatants did not vary significantly between rural and urban respondents, though there was some variation by province and municipality. An interesting finding from a number of focus group discussions, and one that requires further research, regards the possible role played by 'witchcraft'. Several focus group discussions indicated that ex-combatants were sometimes fearful of returning to rural areas because of 'witchcraft'. One focus group of young ex-combatants in Huambo made reference to this, and contrary to the received wisdom, claimed that it was easier to settle in the city:

> ...here in the city one is well received whatever one's circumstances; that does not happen to those that go to the villages because if they have valuable possessions or land they will be submitted to witchcraft. *(Focus Group, Young Ex-combatants, Huambo city, translated by the authors)*

Table 26: Perceptions of Reception in Urban and Rural Areas

Urban or rural	Were you well received by the community?a		Total
	Yes	No	
Rural	89.3%	10.7%	100.0%
Urban	91.2%	8.8%	100.0%
Total	**90.0%**	**10.0%**	**100.0%**

* Data missing in 2 cases, not included here

Graph 23: Right to Training/Jobs in Urban and Rural Areas

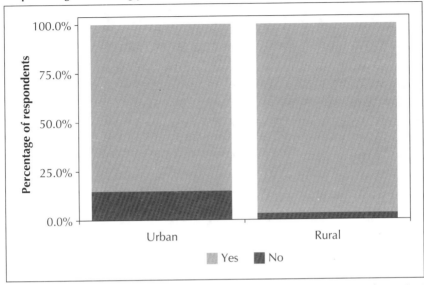

(Question not asked in Huambo Province)

A very strong sense of entitlement to training and jobs was manifested in the survey responses of people in the urban areas (97%) versus a somewhat less pronounced but still significant sense amongst those in the rural areas (85.3%).

General attitudes toward elections did not vary between respondents in the urban or rural areas. The same could be said with respect to political party activism (not pictured), short of actual candidacy. With respect to attitudes towards elections, surveying for a rural-urban divide did not produce any significant results. However, when looking for differences in attitude towards political party participation, it becomes evident that a slightly greater percentage of urban respondents were willing to participate in election campaigns than those in the rural areas.[112]

The difference is more marked when the project inquired whether they were interested in being candidates for office: here 27.3% of the urban-based respondents said they would be interested while only 18.4% of the rural-based respondents said they would. This might be a function of increased exposure to government bureaucracy and related benefits experienced by former combatants in urban areas (particularly because the areas surveyed were provincial capitals), but it could also reflect the fact that farming is a

Table 27: Willingness to Stand as Candidates in Rural and Urban Areas

Urban or rural		Willing to stand as a candidate?		Total
		Yes	No	
Rural	Frequency	69	307	376
	Percent	18.4%	81.6%	100.0%
Urban	Frequency	62	165	227
	Percent	27.3%	72.7%	100.0%
Total	Frequency	131	472	603
	Percent	21.7%	78.3%	100.0%

full-time occupation for many. Those in the wage labour sector of towns and cities are more likely to consider political careers. Again, while the trend is constant, it appears that the highest level of political activism is found in Kuíto – 48% of urban ex-combatants were willing to stand as a candidate, as opposed to just 17% in Huambo or 25% in Huila.

When the rural-urban dimension is correlated with knowledge of political parties, the majority of respondents in both rural and urban areas (70.8%) knew only the major parties, i.e. the MPLA, UNITA and the FNLA. Only a fifth of respondents (18% in rural areas and 21.8% in urban areas) knew the major parties as well as the newer parties.

Table 28: Knowledge of Political Parties in Urban and Rural Areas

Urban or rural	Do you know any political parties?					Total
	MPLA, UNITA, FNLA only	New parties only	MPLA, UNITA, FNLA & new parties	No, none	data missing	
Rural	72.9%	1.1%	16.2%	9.8%	0.0%	100.0%
Urban	67.4%	4.0%	20.3%	7.0%	1.3%	100.0%
Total	70.8%	2.2%	17.7%	8.8%	0.5%	100.0%

Surveying for Economic Standing, Livelihoods and Expectations

A major working hypothesis of the project (and the majority of the literature and policy on reintegration of ex-combatants) is that reintegration depends on the successful establishment of economic livelihoods. This operates on two levels: firstly because sustainable economic livelihoods are seen as a crucial and free-standing element of reintegration, and secondly because economic independence is seen as supporting other elements of social and political reintegration.

As with other population groups in the country, in particular the displaced, the former combatant has yet to achieve a level of economic reintegration which will allow him/her to move beyond current levels of vulnerability. As described above, the former combatant is overly dependent on secondary assistance from humanitarian agencies, and is likely to move between medium vulnerability and high vulnerability depending on whether the agricultural season was good or bad.

While the vast majority of former combatants consider themselves entitled to a job and/or some kind of training, the average ex-combatant is unable to find formal or informal employment. This is because of the overall conditions of the economy and the lack of formal qualifications and training. In this regard, the socio-economic environment in which the ex-combatant finds himself (locally, regionally and nationally) at the time of reintegration is of critical importance – both as an enabler as well as an obstacle to sustainable reintegration (see next chapter for more on this). As correctly noted by the GTZ, 'too little attention has been given thus far to the economic setting in which the war ended and the demobilisation implemented'.[113]

Table 29: Perception of Being Reintegrated, and Receipt of Reintegration Kit and Reintegration Subsidy

| | | Do you consider yourself reintegrated? | |
		Yes	No
Received reintegration kit?	Yes	79.9%	20.1%
	No	72.8%	27.2%
Received reintegration subsidy?	Yes	79.3%	20.7%
	No	74.9%	25.1%

How do economic factors affect former combatant's sense of being reintegrated into society? In order to assess this, the project began by correlating former combatants' sense of reintegration with the provision of emergency reinsertion support at the time of demobilisation (reintegration kit and subsidy) – largely considered a fundamental type of support in the immediate resettlement phase.

As noted in the pages above, monetary reinsertion support plays a critical role in the immediate resettlement period because it is designed to enable the former combatant to ease his reintegration into civilian life. It should be recalled that only 53.1% of the former combatants interviewed confirmed they had received the subsidy – even though this figure did not tally with that obtained through a number of focus group discussions and key informant interviews. As to the demobilisation kit, only 59.7% of respondents had received it.

Although, statistically speaking, no correlation can be inferred on the basis of the data, it does seem that more of those who did not receive reintegration kits and subsidies also do not consider themselves reintegrated – just over a quarter as opposed to one fifth for those who did receive them. Of the total, around 12% did not receive a kit or a subsidy (the proportion is roughly the same in each group) and also reported not feeling reintegrated.

A similar correlation was inferred regarding their sense of reintegration and house ownership. To what extent does owning (as well as renting or loaning) a house contribute to former combatants' sense of being reintegrated? Here the relationship is clearer. As can be seen in table 31, 60% of those without a house (whether owned, rented or loaned) did not consider themselves

Table 30: Perception of Being Reintegrated and House Ownership

House ownership	Do you consider yourself reintegrated?		Total
	Yes	No	
Own house	81.0%	19.0%	273
Belongs to relatives	74.0%	26.0%	77
Rented	72.4%	27.6%	196
Loaned	83.3%	16.7%	48
No house	40.0%	60.0%	5

Table 31: Perception of Being Reintegrated and Main Economic Activity

Main economic activity	Do you consider yourself reintegrated?		Total
	Yes	No	
Occasional wage labour	72.7%	27.3%	128
Agriculture	78.0%	22.0%	328
Informal commerce/trade	80.0%	20.0%	80
Manual trade	87.5%	12.5%	8
Public sector/government employee	85.7%	14.3%	14
Private sector employee	50.0%	50.0%	2
Student	62.5%	37.5%	8
Other	77.8%	22.2%	27
Data missing	80.0%	20.0%	5

reintegrated – although the number of respondents in this category was very small (just five). Firm conclusions could only be derived from a larger sample. This is in sharp contrast to those who either own a house (81%), live in a relative's house (74%) or have a house which is loaned to them (83%).

The project then correlated the respondent's own sense of reintegration with economic standing. As expected, former combatants who have some type of economic activity (in order of importance: manual trade, public sector, informal commerce and agriculture) evidence a high sense of being fully part of the society (70-86%). It is perhaps not surprising that those with permanent formal employment in the public sector are among those with the highest sense of reintegration. Only those with occupations in manual trade show a higher sense of reintegration. The number of ex-combatants formally employed in the private sector is too small for firm conclusions to be drawn (only 2 out of over 600 surveys).

What about former combatants' expectations and sense of being reintegrated? Former combatants' expectations regarding their future livelihoods revealed that finding a job was the most important priority (29% of responses) followed by access to professional training (25%); access to arable land (18%); and continuing their studies (14%). Most notable was that the majority within the sub-group who did not consider themselves reintegrated thought that their expectations on demobilisation had not been met (73%).

In almost all cases, the main reasons given for this were financial and opportunity related (lack of income, lack of qualifications, lack of jobs, lack of training courses). Results from the focus group discussions and key informant interviews added an additional element: the provision of employment and training opportunities is seen as a government responsibility. From Andulo to Chipindo, from Muembessi to Lubango, former combatants continued to wait for the government to provide them with training and jobs. This is largely a function of promises made during the cantonment period. The issue of 'expectations' remains an important component of reintegration, especially when jobs are severely scarce in both the informal and formal markets.

This conclusion is backed up by the responses given to the question 'what could facilitate your reintegration?' Over half the answers were: 'a job', with 'training' the next most common response, given by over a third of ex-combatants. A slightly higher proportion of those who did not consider themselves reintegrated also felt that they were entitled to a job or training (94% versus 87%), but the relationship is not statistically significant and may also simply reflect the fact that this sub-group was less likely to have a job. Of these, 81% felt the government should be responsible for this, 9% NGOs, and only 2% UNITA.

Future plans of the self-assessed 'non-reintegrated' were predominantly to remain where they were (88%), although this may reflect a perception of lack of opportunity more than a choice. If given the opportunity, more than half of them would relocate – most commonly for economic reasons. While there is not a big difference between urban and rural areas in terms of those who would like to move if given the opportunity, a larger proportion of those in rural areas expected to remain where they were, representing half as many again as the number who actually want to stay. A further break-down of ex-combatants' future expectations and plans indicates that another factor (in addition to the perception of opportunity) is the ex-combatant's previous link to the location where he has resettled. Less difference is noted in terms of those who expect to remain (though those in a location they have never lived in before are more likely to expect to move), but the difference (if the opportunity arises) is striking. Over 70% of those who resettled in their birthplace intend to remain there, as opposed to less than half for all other categories.

Surveying for land ownership/access

In the Angolan context, with its preponderance of small scale subsistence agriculture, it is necessary to examine the role of access to land and land ownership in the reintegration process. An obvious problem in doing so is assessing what constitutes ownership, given the customary traditions and the socialist heritage of state intervention. These areas require further investigation. However, based on the data that the project was able to obtain, it would appear that, in certain specific instances, land ownership or access to land does exercise influence over attitudes and participation. This is particularly the case when one narrows the focus and looks at the amount of land held.

In the first instance, however, correlating land ownership and access with perceptions of reintegration does not appear to exercise a significant influence. The sense of being reintegrated is roughly equivalent between those with land or access to it (78.4%) and those without land (73%).

Nevertheless, although there seems to be no significant relationship between the means of access to land (ownership, renting or loan), the quantity does appear to have an effect, as evident in the table below. The more land an ex-combatant has access to, the more likely s/he is to consider him/herself reintegrated into society.

More importantly, lack of land appears to have a direct impact on ex-combatants' perception of their own identity – as civilians, military or demobilised. In fact, only one third of those without access to land saw themselves civilians (34.1%) whereas 57.6% of those with land ownership/access saw themselves as civilians. As the table below shows, there is also an interesting correlation between those who view themselves as 'demobilised'

Table 32: Perceptions of reintgration by land ownership

Land ownership/ access?	Are you reintegrated in civilian life?		Total
	Yes	No	
Yes	78.8%	21.2%	417
No	73.4%	26.6%	185
Total	462	137	599*

* Data missing in 3 cases (not included here)

Table 33: Perceptions of reintegration according to quantity of land to which ex-combatants have access

Quantity of land	Are you reintegrated in civilian life?		Total
	Yes	No	
None	73.4%	26.6%	**184**
Less than one hectare	77.1%	22.9%	**266**
One to two hectares	79.5%	20.5%	**112**
Two or more hectares	89.7%	10.3%	**29**
Total	**77.0%**	**23.0%**	**591***

*   Data missing in 12 cases (not included here)

and land ownership/access in the fact that 64.9% of respondents with no access to or ownership to land still seee themselves as 'demobilised'.

With respect to community reception of ex-combatants, there is an important variance between those with land or access to it (92.8%) and those without (82.7%). Although it is impossible to establish causality, it appears that the way in which an ex-combatant is received by the community may be related to their access to land. It was not within the scope of this survey to probe further into these cases, but previous research on land and reintegration has shown that, while not the norm, a subgroup of ex-combatants returning to rural areas did find themselves denied access to their ancestral land and/or not allocated a new piece of land (Development Workshop, 2004). This may well be what has taken place here – the ex-combatant's perception of having been poorly received may have been linked to land conflicts or lack of available free land for allocation, which has left the ex-combatant landless.

Table 34: Perceptions of identity by land access/ownership

Land ownership/access?	Do you consider yourself ...			Total
	Civilian	Military	Demobilised	
Yes	57.6%	1.0%	41.5%	**417**
No	34.1%	1.1%	64.9%	**185**
Total	**50.3%**	**1.0%**	**48.7%**	**602***

*   Data missing in 1 case (not included here)

Table 35: Reception by community and land access

Land ownership/ access?	Were you well received by the community?		Total
	Yes	No	
Yes	93.0%	7.0%	416
No	83.2%	16.8%	184
Total	90.0%	10.0%	600*

* Data missing in 3 cases (not included here)

In addition, it seems that quantity of land also has an impact here. While a good reception and more land are correlated for lower quantities, those with more than two hectares of land did not feel well received. This may be due to a perception on the part of communities that the ex-combatant had returned 'to take away their land' and might indicate that it is relatively harder for 'wealthier' ex-combatants to reintegrate into communities. This might also be linked to the belief that, in rural areas, 'witchcraft' is likely to be practised against ex-combatants who return with material goods, as explained in focus groups cited above.

In the area of political participation, although attitudes toward elections and rights to vote remained roughly the same, the sense of entitlement to training and jobs increased amongst those without land (see below). This was slightly more pronounced when respondents were asked whether the government was responsible for providing training and jobs. Some 82% of the landless held the government accountable in this area, versus 78% of those with land.

Table 36: Community reception and land access

Quantity of land currently owned	Were you well received by community?		Total
	Yes	No	
None	83.2%	16.8%	184
Less than one hectare	92.9%	7.1%	266
One to two hectares	95.6%	4.4%	113
Two or more hectares	89.7%	10.3%	29
Total	90.2%	9.8%	595*

* Data missing in 8 cases (not included here

Table 37: Membership of political organisations by land ownership/access

Land ownership/ access?	Member of a political organisation		Total
	Yes	No	
Yes	5.8%	94.2%	417
No	10.3%	89.7%	185
Total	7.1%	92.9%	602*

* Data missing in 1 case (not included here)

Table 38: Membership of political organisations by quantity of land

Quantity of land		Member of political organisation?		Total
		Yes	No	
None	Count	19	166	185
	Percent	10.3%	89.7%	100.0%
Less than one hectare	Count	16	251	267
	Percent	6.0%	94.0%	100.0%
One to two hectares	Count	5	108	113
	Percent	4.4%	95.6%	100.0%
Two or more hectares	Count	3	26	29
	Percent	10.3%	89.7%	100.0%
Data missing	Count		8	8
	Percent		100.0%	100.0%
Total	Count	43	559	602
	Percent	7.1%	92.9%	100.0%

More striking is the fact that political organisational membership is twice as high amongst those without land (10.3%) as it is among those with land (5.8%) – a finding that requires further investigation. The rural/urban divide also needs to be factored in because party membership is more common in urban areas, and ex-combatants in urban areas are less dependent on land as a source of their economic livelihoods.

Table 39: Membership of political organisations according to land ownership

Ownership of land		Member of a political organisation?		Total
		Yes	No	
Own land	Frequency	15	322	337
	Percent	4.5%	95.5%	100.0%
Rented	Frequency	1	15	16
	Percent	6.3%	93.8%	100.0%
Loaned	Frequency	8	49	57
	Percent	14.0%	86.0%	100.0%
No land	Frequency	19	166	185
	Percent	10.3%	89.7%	100.0%
Total	**Frequency**	**43**	**552**	**595***
	Percent	**7.2%**	**92.8%**	**100.0%**

* Data missing in 8 cases (not included here)

The quantity of land seems to be significant only in that those with no land and those with more than 2ha are equally likely to be active in political organisations – while those with less than 2ha of land are least likely to be involved.

While this finding might be an anomaly, it could indicate a relationship between economic standing (and in particular poverty) and membership of political organisations. It is interesting to recall the IRI survey in this regard. In that survey, the average profile of party sympathisers and members seems to indicate a correlation between low levels of income and political party membership. 40.8% of party members and 38.5% of party sympathisers were likely to be poor or in a precarious situation (31.3% and 32.5% respectively).[114]

The means by which ex-combatants have access to land also appears to be related to their membership of political organisations, although the numbers renting or being loaned are small so it is hard to draw any definite conclusions. That said, those with no land or who have been loaned land (which implies a more precarious economic situation and/or a land conflict pending resolution) are considerably more likely to be members of political organisations than those who own or rent land.

Surveying for Social Networks

Communities of inclusion and exclusion mediate the experiences of individual ex-combatants, shaping identity formation (and transformation) and influencing the trajectory and utility of the networks in which they participate. This realisation leads us to another guiding assumption of much of the work on reintegration, one borrowed from 'social capital' theory – that individuals who are embedded within associational life, the stuff of 'social capital', are likely to be more knowledgeable as well as active participants in the civil and economic life of the polity.[115]

Social networks are impossible to 'measure' concretely, but they can be inferred through subjective and objective surveys aimed at individuals and members of the community. Three main lines of investigation were pursued: (1) ex-combatants' previous links to community and the presence of family networks; (2) interpersonal relationships (with whom ex-combatants spend their time, to whom they turn for help with problems); and (3) formal membership of community organisations.

The first, that of the 'previous relationship between an ex-combatant and a community', might be expected to affect the way in which the ex-combatant is viewed by the community – an individual returning to his home and family might 'fit in' more easily than an outsider who is easily recognisable

Table 40: Community reception according to previous inhabitance

Previously lived in community	Were you well received by the community?		Total
	Yes	No	
Birthplace	90.5%	9.5%	370
Before military service	93.8%	6.3%	80
During military service	78.6%	21.4%	28
No, never	88.3%	11.7%	120
Total	90.0%	10.0%	598*

* Data missing in 5 cases (not included here)

Table 42: Perceptions of reintegration according to previous links to community

Previously lived in community	Are you reintegrated in civilian life?		Total
	Yes	No	
Birthplace	79.1%	20.9%	369
Before military service	71.3%	28.7%	80
During military service	57.1%	42.9%	28
No, never	80.0%	20.0%	120
Total	**77.2%**	**22.8%**	**597***

*   Data missing in 6 cases (not included here)

as an ex-combatant. However, an equally valid hypothesis is that the reverse may be true – knowledge of an ex-combatant's military past and actions may also prejudice a community against him. From the data, it appears that both may be true. Those returning to their birthplace or somewhere they had previously lived were considerably more likely to be well received than those returning to a place where they had been stationed while with UNITA.

However, while a person in this subgroup consistently appears to be less likely to see himself as reintegrated, resettlement in a place where he has never lived does not appear to be a major obstacle to reintegration. Those who settle in a new place are only marginally less likely to be well received. In addition, they reveal similar perceptions of their own identity and reintegration to respondents who were either born in the community where they have resettled or lived in that community before military service.

This can be partly explained by the fact (established by this and previous DW research in 2004) that most ex-combatants who resettle in a place where they have not previously lived, choose to do so because family relatives live in that place. These family networks significantly increase the probability of ex-combatants being well-received. Again, this backs up previous research by DW that showed family networks were crucial to enabling ex-combatants in rural areas to obtain land on arrival – surely a major part of a 'good reception'. Focus groups also indicated, almost universally, that the existence of family networks was the major factor enabling ex-combatants to find employment, followed by possession of documentation, and money to pay small bribes/buy presents (in Angola know as *'gasosa'*).

Table 43: Community reception according to presence of family

Do you have family here?	Were you well received by the community?		Total
	Yes	No	
Yes	92.3%	7.7%	**494**
No	80.2%	19.8%	**106**
Total	**90.2%**	**9.8%**	**600***

* Data missing in 3 cases (not included here)

However, the effect of family networks on ex-combatants perceptions of whether or not they are reintegrated cannot be considered significant - additional factors must therefore be at play determining ex-combatant's own perception of reintegration. It is worth noting that communities reveal a certain degree of ambivalence towards ex-military personnel when probed during focus group discussions. While most profess that there is no particular difference between ex-combatants and other members of the community, when asked whether they would prefer to employ an ex-soldier or a civilian (or if there was no difference), all said they would hire the civilian.

The importance of trust comes to the fore once again. As noted throughout this monograph, trust is of critical importance for the successful reintegration of former combatants within communities in their chosen areas of resettlement. The considerable disagreement in academic circles as to the relative importance of trust in the development of social capital notwithstanding (in particular theories which emphasise the associational network component of social capital), this is a very important variable and one that must be taken into account.[116]

In fact, an ex-combatant's previous ties to a community are also a very strong influence on their future plans and hopes. Ex-combatants were asked whether they expected to remain in their current location in the future, and then, whether, if given the opportunity, they would prefer to stay or to move. More details on the reasons for each choice were also gathered. From the data, it seems that the vast majority (96%) of those who have returned to their birthplace expect to stay, versus 75% who have settled in a place where they have never lived before. More striking still is their preference if the choice were available – 70% of those in their birthplace would still choose to remain, but almost half of all the others would actually prefer to move. Resettlement in the place of origin does, therefore, seem to make an ex-combatant considerably more likely to want to remain there.

There is some distortion introduced here since ex-combatants not returning to their place of origin appear to be more commonly found in urban areas (35% of the urban population as opposed to 11% of the rural), whereas in rural areas surveyed, 77% had returned to their place of origin (37% in urban areas). There is also a significant difference in most cases between the preferences of ex-combatants in urban and rural areas (see table below).

In addition, while it still appears that resettling in the place of origin is a significant factor – since in both urban and rural areas around 70% would chose to remain – it also seems that for other groups, who do not have ties of ancestry and birthright, there is no strong preference to remain or stay if resettled in an urban area. In fact, the majority of these would rather move away from communities in rural areas. This does appear to suggest that ties of kinship and birthright are an important factor in binding an ex-combatant

Table 44: Previous Links to Community and Intentions to Remain

Previous links to community		Would stay given the choice (%)	Expect to stay (%)	Total cases
Birthplace	Rural	70.5	96.9	287
	Urban	69.9	91.6	83
	Total	**70.4**	**95.7**	**370**
Before military service	Rural	29.0	83.9	31
	Urban	51.0	83.3	48
	Total	**42.5**	**83.5**	**79**
During military service	Rural	50.0	92.9	14.0
	Urban	42.9	78.6	14
	Total	**46.4**	**85.7**	**28**
Never	Rural	33.3	81.0	42
	Urban	53.2	71.8	78
	Total	**46.2**	**75.0**	**120**

to a community, and make them more likely to choose to resettle over the medium to long term.[117]

While the presence of family networks and previous ties to a community are relatively easy to identify, the less visible ties of acquaintance and friendship, which are an equally valid part of social capital, are harder to test for. Ex-combatants were asked with whom they generally spent their time, and to whom they turn for help with problems. As noted, former combatants tended to spend more time with their families (442 responses) followed by other former combatants (178 responses), and with fellow church members (143 responses). We found that, in general, who ex-combatants spend their time with is not a significant factor when correlated against their own perceptions of reintegration – regardless of whom they spent time with, around 75% considered themselves reintegrated.

When asked who they turned to for help with problems, there is no clear correlation in terms of perceptions of reintegration although certain responses stand out: those who would turn to a government representative (usually the administrator) are the most likely to also consider themselves reintegrated (85%), while those who would turn to a UNITA representative are the least likely to consider themselves as reintegrated (71%).

Overall, however, there is little difference between those who do consider themselves reintegrated and those who do not, or between 'civilians' and 'demobilised' in terms of who they would turn to. In all cases, around half the ex-combatants would turn to the *Soba,* and the remainder are divided between the family (around 30%), the church (around 10%), and friends (around 8%), with only a small minority selecting political representatives (around 4% each for government and UNITA). Perceptions of authority also appear to be only selectively related to the degree of reintegration of ex-combatants. Some 91% of those who thought the

Table 45: Perception of Being Reintegrated and Principal Source of Information

| Are you reintegrated in civilian life? | UNITA representative a principal source of information? | | Total |
	Yes	No	
Yes	58.5%	78.5%	**77.2%**
No	41.5%	21.5%	**22.8%**

Table 46: Views on elections vs. information sources available

| Principal source of information | Do you think elections are important to consolidate peace? | | | | Total | |
| | Yes | | No | | | |
	Frequency	Percent	Frequency	Percent	Frequency	Percent
Soba	69	92.0	3	4.0	75	100.0
Government representative	21	100.0	0	0.0	21	100.0
MPLA representative	3	100.0	0	0.0	3	100.0
UNITA representative	41	100.0	0	0.0	41	100.0
Radio	492	97.8	8	1.6	503	100.0
Newspaper	18	100.0	0	0.0	18	100.0
Television	22	95.7	0	0.0	23	100.0
Other	17	100.0	0	0.0	17	100.0
None	3	60.0	0	0.0	5	100.0
Total	585	97.0	11	1.8	603	100.0

* 7 cases of data missing excluded here

Table 47: Identity Perceptions according to organisational membership and Municipality

Municipality	Member of an organisation?	Do you consider yourself...			Total
		Civilian	Military	Demobilised	
Lubango	Yes	34.5%		65.5%	29
	No	36.2%		63.8%	47
	Total	35.5%		64.5%	76
Chipindo	Yes	62.7%		37.3%	75
	No	54.0%		46.0%	50
	Total	59.2%		40.8%	125
Vila Nova	Yes	50.0%		50.0%	32
	No	57.6%	1.5%	40.9%	66
	Total	55.1%	1.0%	43.9%	98
Huambo Sede	Yes	66.7%		33.3%	18
	No	60.5%		39.5%	76
	Total	61.7%		38.3%	94
Kuito	Yes	41.2%		58.8%	17
	No	57.9%	5.3%	36.8%	38
	Total	52.7%	3.6%	43.6%	55
Andulo	Yes	50.0%		50.0%	48
	No	34.3%	2.9%	62.7%	102
	Total	39.3%	2.0%	58.7%	150

Table 48: Perceptions of Identity by Organisational Membership

Do you consider yourself ...	Member of a political organisation		Member of a religious organisation	
	Yes	No	Yes	No
Civilian	41.9%	51.1%	53.2%	49.3%
Military	0.0%	1.1%	0.0%	1.4%
Demobilised	58.1%	47.9%	46.8%	49.3%
Total	100.0%	100.0%	100.0%	100.0%

administrator the most important figure in the community also considered themselves reintegrated – as opposed to 77% of the overall caseload. Overall, the *Soba* is still considered the most important figure in the community regardless of ex-combatants' perceptions of their own identity or reintegration.

The figure of the UNITA representative appears in answers to the question on which information sources ex-combatants have access to. It seems that those who claimed that a UNITA representative was among their main sources of information are also less likely to consider themselves reintegrated.

The figure of 59% – those for whom a UNITA representative was a principal source of information who also consider themselves reintegrated – can also be compared with 86% of those who named a government representative. Thus, the sources of information to which ex-combatants have access do seem to have an influence on their perceptions of their own reintegration.

When one correlates opinions on elections with information source, it emerges that slightly less than 5% of those who cite the *soba* and radio as their primary sources believe elections are not important.

Finally, moving on to more formal criteria, membership (or not) of an organisation did not seem to have any significant effect on respondents' sense of being reintegrated. However, upon breakdown by municipality, a more complicated picture emerges. Statistically, the relationship is only significant in Andulo, where 50% of those who were members of an organisation saw themselves as civilians, whereas only 34% of those who were not saw them selves as civilians. The implication is that ex-combatants who are members of an organisation are more likely to see themselves as civilians.

In Kuito there is also an apparent relationship, because 41% who are members of organisations consider themselves reintegrated, as opposed to a higher 58% of those who are not – i.e. the relationship is reversed. In this area, ex-combatants who are members of organisations are less likely to see themselves as civilians.

The variations can perhaps be explained by the type of organisation ex-combatants are members of. For instance, being a member of an organisation composed of demobilised soldiers might be unlikely to predispose ex-combatants to regard themselves as civilians. Being a member of a church or a non-political, community-based organisation might assist in reintegrating

Table 49: Perceptions of reintegration by organisational membership

Reintegrated in civilian life?	Member of a political organisation		Member of a religious organisation	
	Yes	No	Yes	No
Yes	67.4%	77.9%	80.7%	75.8%
No	32.6%	22.1%	19.3%	24.2%
Total	100.0%	100.0%	100.0%	100.0%

an ex-combatant and breaking down a militarised identity. In support of this theory, Kuíto, in which organisational membership predisposes an ex-combatant to consider themselves as a demobilised, also shows the highest level of membership of political organisations – one in eight. And although Andulo is not far behind, it stands out as exhibiting a strong correlation (valid in Andulo alone) between church/religious organisation membership and a civilian identity (see below). In Andulo, it appears that ex-combatant who are a members of a church or religious organisation (as almost two thirds are) are roughly twice as likely to see themselves as a civilian as those who are non-church members. In Kuíto, on the other hand, the relationship between churches and reintegration is not significant.

The question 'do you consider you are reintegrated into civilian life' does not produce identical results to the identity question, and there is once again no straightforward correlation with organisational membership at the aggregate level. A breakdown by organisational type produces more useful results.

Some variation by municipality does seem to exist. Generally, membership of a religious organisation does appear to be an advantage in terms of reintegration across the different regions, except in Vila Nova where the relationship is, for some reason, reversed. However when church membership is checked for instead of religious organisation, the relationship in Vila Nova weakens and becomes insignificant.

Political membership generally seems to follow the trend shown above – linked to weaker feelings of reintegration and the 'demobilised identity'. However, while it has a particularly strong impact in Andulo, the relationship is reversed in Lubango. No demobilised soldiers were members of political organisations in Huambo city, so it is difficult to establish whether this is an urban/rural trend, or has another basis.

Table 50: Perceptions of reintegration by membership of political organisations (by Municipality)

Municipality		Are you reintegrated in civilian life?		
		Yes	No	Total
Andulo	Yes	53.3%	46.7%	15
	No	78.7%	21.3%	136
	Total	76.2%	23.8%	151
Chipindo	Yes	83.3%	16.7%	12
	No	89.5%	10.5%	114
	Total	88.9%	11.1%	126
Huambo Sede	No	72.6%	27.4%	95
	Total	72.6%	27.4%	95
Kuito	Yes	57.1%	42.9%	7
	No	65.3%	34.7%	49
	Total	64.3%	35.7%	56
Lubango	Yes	85.7%	14.3%	7
	No	77.9%	22.1%	68
	Total	78.7%	21.3%	75
Vila Nova	Yes	50.0%	50.0%	2
	No	74.7%	25.3%	95
	Total	74.2%	25.8%	97

% within Political organisation

Ex-combatants who were members of an organisation did not exhibit particularly different responses to those who weren't when it came to community reception. Attitudes towards elections also did not vary significantly according to organisational membership – especially given that virtually the entire survey group viewed elections as important and believed they had the right to vote as Angolan citizens. The survey also showed little difference in the level of knowledge of political parties when general organisational membership was checked for.

Surveying for Military Rank

In the course of interrogating the data for significant correlations, the role of military rank has sometimes been suggested as an important factor in determining attitude towards reintegration. Indeed, some work on reintegration in other settings has suggested that under certain circumstances, middle ranking officers who are dissatisfied with the outcomes of peace might constitute a significant threat. This is because they have the know-how and are ideally positioned to find and command the loyalty of former combatants' networks (towards a renewal of hostilities but also criminal aims). The general picture one gets of the influence of rank is that the middle ranking officers have a much stronger sense of a shared outlook on a variety of issues relating to reintegration.

Self-perceptions of reintegration, as seen through the divisions within the military, do appear to vary, varying from 50% of the colonels defining themselves as 'civilians' to 53.3% of the privates defining themselves as 'civilians' (40% of colonels and lieutenant colonels when the two ranks are combined). The lowest rates are to be found amongst middle ranking

Table 51: Perception of Being Reintegrated and Military Rank

Military Rank	Reintegrated in civilian life?		Total
	Yes	No	
Colonel	75.0%	25.0%	4
Lieutenant-colonel	0.0%	100.0%	1
Major	55.0%	45.0%	20
Captain	71.1%	28.9%	77
Lieutenant	77.7%	22.3%	238
Warrant officer	88.0%	12.0%	84
Sergeant	78.8%	21.2%	53
Private	75.8%	24.2%	120
Unspecified/ other	83.3%	16.7%	6
Total	77.2%	22.8%	603

Table 52: Perception of Reception by the Community and Military Rank

Military rank	Were you well received by the community?		Total
	Yes	No	
Colonel	100.0%	.0%	4
Lieutenant-colonel	100.0%	.0%	1
Major	95.0%	5.0%	20
Captain	88.2%	11.8%	77
Lieutenant	88.2%	11.8%	238
Warrant officer	90.5%	9.5%	84
Sergeant	88.7%	11.3%	53
Private	94.2%	5.8%	120
Unspecified/other	83.3%	16.7%	6
Total	**90.0%**	**10.0%**	**603**

officers (lieutenant-colonel, majors and captains), of whom a majority see themselves as 'demobilised' rather than as 'civilians'.

The table above shows that majors are the least likely to feel reintegrated into civilian life, at only 55% versus rates of 70% and 80% amongst other ranks. As with the overall responses to this survey question, which found that a quarter of all ex-soldiers surveyed did not characterise themselves as civilians, these findings could be interpreted as lending weight to the view that this category of officer is especially volatile (i.e. prone to dissatisfaction). It is also worth noting that one alternative explanation for these responses is that senior officers interpreted the category of 'demobilised' as reflecting the formal situation in which they found themselves – that is to say, they had not been pensioned off but are rather 'in the reserves' at the time of the survey.

Focus group discussions with high/middle-ranking officers in Andulo, for example, revealed the following view of reintegration:

...a former combatant ceases to be a former combatant when he is totally part of society – that is, when he can find a *certain* job and his children go to school [our emphasis].

For these former combatants then, the fact that the majority of them are
unemployed, may be directly correlated with the absence of civilian status.
A similar view was expressed by the high/middle-ranking officers' focus
group in the commune of Mitcha, Lubango, Huíla province. They believed
that much depended on each combatant's economic independence.

The reception experienced by the different military personnel varies, hovering
around 90% in almost every instance. This is interesting when compared
to the focus group material (Lubango; Chipindo) in which key informants
representing UNITA stated categorically that there were numerous cases
of discrimination by local officials in the provision of housing, jobs, etc.
Perhaps a distinction needs to be made between the public's reception of
the ex-combatants and that of government officials.

Regarding entitlement to training and a job, the statistics on military rank
and sense of entitlement do not elicit significant differences from the general
findings. But, when asked who should provide these, the higher ranking
officers are clearer (100%) in assigning responsibility to the government.
Here again, the majors stand out as holding a distinctively different position

Table 53: Attitude to Jobs/Training by Military Rank

Military rank	Do you have the right to training & jobs?		Total
	Yes	No	
Colonel	100.0%	.0%	4
Lieutenant-colonel	100.0%	.0%	1
Major	87.5%	12.5%	20
Captain	96.4%	3.6%	77
Lieutenant	90.9%	9.1%	238
Warrant officer	88.2%	11.8%	84
Sergeant	85.0%	15.0%	53
Private	81.3%	18.7%	120
Unspecified/other	100.0%	.0%	6
Total	**89.0%**	**11.0%**	**603**

Table 54: Expectations at the Time of Demobilisation and Military Rank

Military Rank	Principal desire/expectation at the time of demobilisation(a)								Total no. Respondents
	Study	Training	Job	Housing	Land	Find family	Secure peace	Other	
Colonel	25.0%	50.0%	50.0%	0.0%	0.0%	0.0%	0.0%	0.0%	4
Lieutenant-colonel	0.0%	0.0%	0.0%	0.0%	0.0%	100.0%	0.0%	0.0%	1
Major	20.0%	40.0%	30.0%	5.0%	20.0%	5.0%	5.0%	5.0%	20
Captain	13.0%	31.2%	39.0%	5.2%	24.7%	2.6%	1.3%	1.3%	77
Lieutenant	13.9%	29.8%	31.9%	6.3%	29.4%	5.9%	0.0%	2.1%	238
Warrant officer	20.2%	19.0%	31.0%	2.4%	39.3%	9.5%	0.0%	0.0%	84
Sergeant	24.5%	28.3%	22.6%	1.9%	39.6%	3.8%	0.0%	1.9%	53
Private	26.7%	18.3%	18.3%	5.0%	46.7%	11.7%	0.0%	0.8%	120
Unspecified/other	16.7%	33.3%	33.3%	0.0%	16.7%	50.0%	0.0%	0.0%	6
Total	18.4%	26.5%	29.2%	4.8%	33.8%	7.5%	0.3%	1.5%	603

Respondents sometimes gave more than one answer. Percentages reflect the proportion of the ex-combatants of a particular rank who gave that response.

to the rest: only 50% believe that the government should be responsible and they assign the highest figure (25%) to the NGO community.

Looking at the data for which expectations are held by different ranks suggests that lower ranks (privates) had particular expectations of receiving land upon being demobilised. By contrast, middle-ranking officers had higher expectations of training and education. When it comes to whether they believed their desires for demobilisation had been realised, well over a third of all ranks said these had not been met. And, arguably most important of all, the senior ranks were nearly universal in designating the government as responsible for providing jobs and training, while figures are nearly as high for the lower ranks.

CHAPTER 5

FROM SOLDIERS TO CITIZENS
Concluding Thoughts

Introduction

The aim of the project was to develop a comprehensive assessment of the reintegration experience, and potential sources of influence on that experience, amongst ex-UNITA combatants in three of the most contested provinces in the Angolan civil war. To arrive at this, the project team surveyed for economic, social and political indicators that would illuminate key areas of the reintegration process. Five aspects of the reintegration process in particular emerged from analysis of the quantitative and qualitative data, namely (i) reintegration and vulnerability: former combatants and other vulnerable groups; (ii) reintegration and identity; (iii) reintegration and social capital; (iv) reintegration and sustainable livelihoods; and, finally, (v) reintegration and political participation.

Reintegration and Vulnerability: Former Combatants and Other Vulnerable Groups

One of the objectives was to use the data gathered *in situ* to reflect critically on whether former combatants' experience of reintegration was different enough (from other vulnerable groups in post-conflict environments) to justify targeted reintegration programmes. As noted, the rationale behind reintegration programmes has often been based on the need to adequately address the particular needs of ex-combatants so that the risks of a possible return to war and/ or a rise in criminality are minimised.[118] However, in both policy and academic circles, the dispute about targeted and therefore differentiated reintegration support to former combatants is far from resolved. While few people doubt the need for adequate demobilisation and reinsertion support in the immediate return/resettlement phases, there is very little agreement on targeted support for what in essence is a slow, multidimensional and complex process.

Reflecting on the reintegration of former combatants in Liberia, Kees Kingma encapsulates the two sides of the argument particularly well. On one side of the argument:

...reasons for not targeting the assistance to the ex-combatants were, among others: that so many more people were displaced and affected by the war; the general perception that ex-combatants should not be further rewarded; the fact that it was hard to define who is an ex-combatant and who is not; and the fact that because of atrocities committed, the ex-combatants themselves do not want to admit that they were'.

On the other side of the argument,

...there are, however, arguments for at least some direct support for reintegration of ex-soldiers and guerrillas, namely (1) from a humanitarian point of view; (2) as compensation for sacrifices and loss of educational opportunities; (3) because of their potential contribution to general development; (4) because failed reintegration of armed ex-combatants could jeopardise the peace-building process'.[119]

First and foremost, it should be noted that each post-conflict situation presents its own unique profile with specific challenges – conflicts have unique histories and aetiologies, actor types and strategies, severity and scope of consequences. Demobilisation and reintegration programmes must therefore be very carefully tailored to the needs of the societies in which they are implemented rather than being based on a 'one size fits all' blueprint. This realisation has, in the past decade, gradually filtered through to policy and implementing agencies; witness the very different approaches to demobilisation and reintegration adopted, for example, in Burundi and the DRC, as well as the importance attached to context by large funds such as the World Bank's MDRP or development agencies such as the GTZ.[120]

We therefore tend to avoid general prescriptions as to the question of targeted reintegration support to former combatants. What the analysis makes patently clear, however, is that in post-conflict situations where the socio-economic fabric of society has been damaged beyond recognition, and in which large numbers of civilians find themselves living precariously from one day to the next (as families of military personnel, as internally displaced peoples, as refugees), their vulnerability profile seems to have more in common with those of the former combatant than would perhaps be the case in other situations.

In the Angolan case, these different groups 'descended' simultaneously on the local level, through more or less controlled processes of resettlement and return. From a research point of view, this had the benefit of allowing for a better understanding of the different needs of the various groups and, perhaps more importantly, of the way they interacted with one another in a post-conflict context characterised by severe scarcity of resources.

It is important to restate that our focus has been on the reintegration process – from an economic, social and political point of view. It goes without saying that by their very decision to cease fighting and agree to a cease-fire, to demobilise and disarm, former combatants (of all ranks and in all contexts) played the decisive role in the sustainability of peace processes. After all, they are the primary perpetrators of violence, their own justifications for doing so notwithstanding. Whether a war's ending comes through a negotiated peace agreement where none of the parties has reached a decisive advantage in the battlefield, an outright military victory of one party or coalition of parties against another, an international peace enforcement operation, or any other means, demobilisation, disarmament and reintegration support for resettlement and return plays a fundamental role in peace-building and, therefore, long-term development. In fact, successful reintegration of former combatants in the long term is inextricably linked to the way in which processes of demobilisation and disarmament are conducted in the immediate post-war period.

The circumstances of the end of war in Angola were described in chapter one, as were the type of forces to be demobilised and their trajectory during the last phase of the war. At the same time we attempted to give a glimpse of Angola's post-war emergency, which constituted the context within which this last attempt at DD&R was implemented – a context characterised by a humanitarian crisis without precedent. More than a third of its population internally displaced and several thousand refugees in neighbouring countries; there was limited or no accessibility to large parts of the country; overcrowding in urban areas and thousands of people in temporary resettlement sites, not to mention the state of the country's infrastructure (road networks but also health and education facilities). The situation was so severe that, during 2002, the UN conducted the largest and most expensive of its operations in Angola.

At the time the demobilisation and reintegration process began, more than a million civilians were being assisted by the humanitarian community present in the country – with an unspecified, yet much greater number, in need of emergency nutrition and health care assistance. With the quartering process underway, and with thousands of combatants making their way to the quartering areas, it became increasingly clear that the families of combatants also required assistance – the allowance by the government to permit former combatants' family members to gather in satellite reception areas was extremely important because it opened the way for humanitarian agencies to quickly stabilise this large population group (numbering more than 300,000). In the specific context in which the war ended, this decision was widely praised by all actors involved, including UNITA.

Following demobilisation, former combatants began their return and resettlement process, thereby joining several million civilian Angolans who were doing exactly the same, either through controlled and organised processes or spontaneously. When the project arrived in the central plateau of Angola to conduct survey research, two years had passed since the end of the war and, in the three provinces, in both urban and rural locations, the bulk of resettlement and return was underway. With very few exceptions, the project found that no significant levels of localised conflict between the different groups had occurred (in particular between residents, returnees and former combatants) – a finding substantiated by empirical research conducted by other organisations such as Development Workshop and Care.

Two questions arise when researching differentiated support: (1) Do former combatants require, because of their specificity – a function of their role and experience during war as well as their expectations following demobilisation – a different approach to reintegration support (whether or not associated with the perception of possible risks posed by this target group)?; (2) Is differentiated support required as a result of former combatants' different profile (as regards vulnerability, economic standing, skills, etc) to that of other target groups, and in particular the displaced?

We will begin by discussing the second question. As discussed in chapter 3, former combatants largely chose to resettle in areas where they had previous ties, either because it was their place of origin or to join family members. By and large, the former combatant and by extension his family (averaging nine members) was well received in the community of return/resettlement. With little or no formal education and professional training (either before joining or during his time with UNITA[121]), more than half of the sample returned to small-scale farming (their primary activity before joining UNITA), or began working in various types of wage labour (particularly in urban areas) and trade in the informal economy. Moreover, the project found that, as with other population groups and in particular the returnee and resettled population, the former combatant had yet to achieve a level of economic reintegration that would allow him to move beyond medium to high vulnerability, where he remained largely dependent on food aid. In all these aspects, the former combatant is remarkably similar to other vulnerable groups.[122]

Upon arrival, the former combatant was likely to find that more than half the community was made up of returnees (45%) and resettled households (3.7%). Only 48.4% of households had lived in that community for an extended period. In addition, and of note to the issue at hand, was that 'only in 40% of the communities with long-term residents and newcomers, are long-term residents better off than recently settled households, in particular with respect to the condition and size of dwellings and access to productive assets (ploughs, etc). For other characteristics, such as access to luxury goods, access to income-generating activities and knowledge of farming practices, there are almost no differences (not significant). Incidences where resettled households are better off than residents are 'very rare.'[123]

What is perhaps significant is the remarkable (though not surprising) similarity in livelihood strategies. In fact, for the former combatant as for all other groups (residents, resettled, returned), agriculture remains the single most important economic activity, followed by casual labour, livestock, charcoal production, and various business-related activities. Although it is gradually improving, the vulnerability of all of these groups to difficult agricultural seasons has been a constant in the immediate post-war period. Similarly, during difficult times, the coping strategies and mechanisms used in rural Angola are the same as those of former combatants – these can be seen in the graph below.

Graph 24: Relative Importance of Coping Strategies in Angola[124]

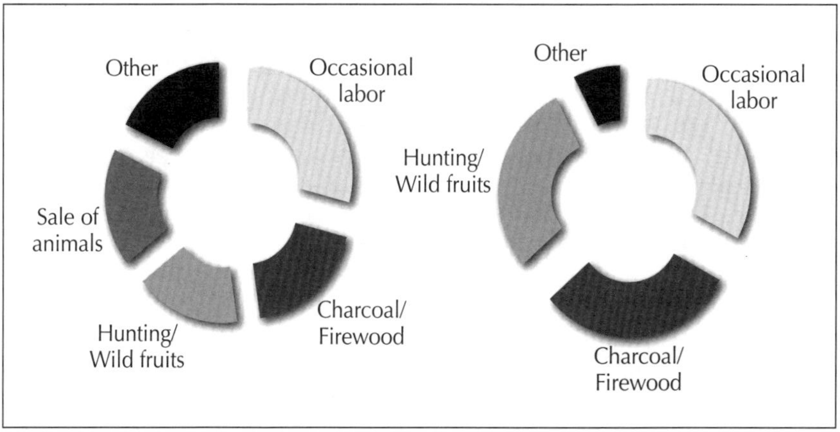

All these groups face the same limited choices, a combined result of lack of income diversification and access to basic services. In addition, 'the loss of productive and domestic assets during the war, the limited labour market in rural areas, and the low crop yields in the past few years in some areas continues to affect the productive capacities of the returnee population'.[125] In Angola, the scale of resettlement and return of all population groups was such that it represents the single most important dynamic during the immediate post-war period. Upon arrival, all population groups face the same limitations to restoring their livelihoods and all require substantial levels of humanitarian assistance. In fact, as noted by the WFP and partners, "it is during the first years of resettlement that these households need support from the humanitarian community in combination with the repair and reconstruction of the transport, school and health infrastructures by the government and its partners".[126]

It is therefore clear that, in this case, there is little that distinguishes the former combatant from other vulnerable groups – they face the same challenges, experience a very similar degree of vulnerability, are equipped with the same very limited set of skills, and survive using identical income-generating activities. What of the argument that because of their specificity former combatants require a differentiated approach to reintegration support? Could it primarily be related to the perception of possible risks posed by this target group if not properly attended to?

In general, and irrespective of the circumstances within which combatants give up their arms and agree to demobilise, the idea is that they need to feel that they have achieved something if they are to continue to abide by the rules of peace.[127] As noted by the Praxis Group, "when combatants are asked to give up their arms, they face a "point of no return": they and their leaders must have faith in a future where the advantages of peace outweigh those of war".[128] This argument seems to find practical evidence in many failed peace processes, where the combined effect of inadequate DD&R programmes and the failure to address root or structural causes of conflict (inequality, discriminatory political institutions, poverty and underdevelopment, etc) form the ideal ingredients of a resurgence of violence, often with former combatants at the helm – their military-related skills and mobilisation potential being critical factors in this regard.

At the time the war ended in Angola, UNITA was largely destroyed as a military force and had few options but to "negotiate". With an average of 17 years in the movement's military forces, a great part of which were spent in active combat, its soldiers and officers had little choice but to negotiate – the only real option available to the top leadership of the movement following Jonas Savimbi´s death. Their choice led to the resumption of the Lusaka process and ultimately led to the extinction of the military component of UNITA. It is probable that by the time the MoU was signed in Luanda during April 2002, the bulk of UNITA's forces longed for peace as much as Angolan civilians did – after all, the relentless offensive mounted by the FAA and the effect of sanctions imposed on UNITA had driven the military wing of the movement close to annihilation. The images of UNITA soldiers emerging from the bush en route to quartering areas and the dire condition in which they arrived are clear evidence of this. Consequently, there was no real risk of a return to war in the short term. Yet it is unquestionable that the long-term success of peacebuilding and democratisation in Angola depends on the participation of all – particularly of those who were directly involved in military activities.[129] Former combatants' perception of their place in a peaceful society is therefore critical – and it is this that leads us to the question of reintegration and identity.

Reintegration and Identity

The centrality of identity is well recognised by scholars and policy makers alike to be crucial to the process of reintegration. What is striking about the Angolan case, at least as presented through the findings of this project, is the degree to which former UNITA soldiers did not see themselves to be fully 'civilianised'. With nearly half characterising themselves as either 'demobilised' (48.6%) or 'military' (1%), it is evident that despite it being more than two years since the formal ending of the civil war and a further 10 months after their arrival in their current place of residence, many of the ex-soldiers surveyed still hold non-civilian identities.

Why they feel this way is not particularly illuminated through an analysis of the former combatants' view of their reception by host communities. Contrary to what one would expect, the vast majority of the ex-soldiers believe that they were in fact well-received by their respective host communities. One facet of this can be explained by the numbers of respondents who settled in or near their place of origin, where most claim they have familial ties. However, as noted above, focus group interviews provide a somewhat contradictory account of the experience of reception, presenting anecdotal evidence of persistent discrimination by local government and MPLA party officials on the basis of the ex-soldiers' political affiliation. If this latter experience has been the case, then perhaps this provides a partial explanation for the persistence of the military identity despite the positive reception from family.

Another hypothesis is that the ex-soldiers are actually actively mobilising – not in the military sense but rather the social and perhaps even political sense – around the UNITA banner as a socio-economic strategy in light of the adverse conditions they faced immediately upon demobilising (see below). And finally, it is also possible – as suggested by some ex-combatants in focus groups – that the demobilised identity is a label both attached by communities in a pejorative sense and instrumentalised by ex-combatants to attract economic support from organisations including the government and NGOs. In the end, additional corroborative evidence is needed for a more complete reckoning of this phenomenon.

A number of identity-based factors which may have been expected to have a big impact do not, in the end, seem all that significant – ex-combatants of all ages, ethnicities, gender, religions, and backgrounds seem to experience varying levels of difficulty in reintegrating at roughly equivalent levels. There are some geographical variations, perhaps indicating that some environments have proved more difficult to reintegrate into than others, although there is no real evidence on the basis of this survey data as to why this may be the case. The fact that ex-combatants in rural areas are more likely to consider themselves reintegrated (80% versus 73%, which is significant at the 5% level but the difference is not large) may be attributable to having better access to employment, housing and land.

While other sources of identity such as gender and religion were not seen to be strongly correlated to perceptions of reintegration, aspects of the experience of military service with UNITA appears to have played a role in shaping ex-soldiers' perceptions of reintegration. For example, the longer ex-combatants spent away from home and family and with UNITA, the less likely they are to now consider themselves as 'civilians', more often opting for the label 'demobilised'. The link is not definitive, however – even among those who spent over 20 years with UNITA, some 46% still see themselves as 'civilians', versus 57% of those who spent less than 10 years with UNITA. Perhaps related to this, the younger ex-combatants also appear slightly more likely to view themselves as civilians, although, once again, the relationship is not definitive.

Rank within UNITA appears to have been a more important factor (although of course in many cases this is related to the time spent in UNITA). Although the small number who said they still considered themselves as 'military' makes overall statistical analysis more difficult, there does appear to be a significant correlation between ex-combatants' former rank and their current perception of themselves. The number who chose 'military' as an identity is so low that no real conclusions can be drawn from it. However, those of higher rank are less likely to see themselves as civilians and remain attached to their status as 'demobilised', which implies a persistent attachment to their former military status, and thus a degree of separation from the communities that surround them.

Whether or not an ex-combatant has previously been demobilised may also be a significant factor, making it less likely that an ex-combatant will feel he has reintegrated successfully – although, even so, the majority did consider that they had reintegrated (71%). It is noticeable that of those who did not think they had successfully reintegrated, 82% also saw themselves as 'demobilised' rather than as civilians.

Generally speaking, the previous relationship between an ex-combatant and a community does not, surprisingly, seem to be important. Those living in a place to which they have no previous ties are just as likely to feel reintegrated and consider themselves civilians as those who have returned to their village of birth. However, the subgroup of those living who now live where they were stationed during their time with UNITA stand out. They are less likely to have been well received by the community following demobilisation (78% versus a global average of 90%). They appear to be much more likely to hold onto their 'demobilised' identity (36% consider themselves civilians versus an overall average of 50%), and much less likely to consider themselves reintegrated into civilian life (57% versus a global average of 77%).

As might be expected, those who feel they were not well received by the community are also less likely to now consider themselves to be reintegrated. Of those who were not well received, less than two thirds saw themselves as reintegrated, as opposed to almost four fifths of those who were well received. However, it should be remembered that the two are not automatically linked – 85% of those who did not consider themselves reintegrated said that they had, nevertheless, been well-received by the communities in which they were residing; and one third of those who were poorly received do now nevertheless see themselves as reintegrated.

In addition, it must be remembered that a poor reception for an ex-combatant may be – although not always – due to factors such as their past actions during the war (looting and destruction of property, physical abuse, violence and even killing was not uncommon during the war) and so the community certainly cannot be automatically held 'responsible' for the success or failure of an ex-combatant to reintegrate. The particularly poor reception given to ex-combatants who were known to a community in their military capacity suggests that this, even if not elaborated upon by the ex-combatant, may be an important factor.

The relationship between civil-military identity and expectations of employment and training is telling, with the overwhelming majority of individuals who declared themselves to be civilians having very high expectations (91.6%), while those who saw themselves as demobilised (86.9%) and military (80%) held somewhat lower expectations. Meeting those expectations, given that the ex-soldiers believe the government is responsible for these provisions, is clearly an important dimension of the reintegration process for former combatants. The cost of disappointment, however, may not be as high (at least at this stage) as this may imply. In the end, only 4% of those ex-soldiers who did not consider themselves reintegrated had actually considered a return to military life.

Reintegration and Social Capital

According to Francis Fukuyama: 'social capital is important to the efficient functioning of modern economies, and is the *sine qua non* of stable liberal democracy.'[130] Information flows and norms of reciprocity constitute the material (albeit somewhat intangible) basis for social capital, which is itself employed to create and sustain group identities that form that basis for collective action. The twin expressions of social capital – 'bonding' and 'bridging' – underscore the differing impact that collective action can have in a society.[131] Bonding strategies, sometimes characterised as vertical networks, build on group affinities to establish a 'radius of trust' to the detriment of those defined as outside the group. In contrast, bridging strategies are horizontal networks that foster links across groups, creating 'positive externalities' that spill over into the wider society.

From an economic perspective, the primary function of social capital is to reduce the transaction costs associated with business and public activity. The state is widely acknowledged to have limited capacity, through public policy means, to generate social capital.[132] However, the role of the state is seen to be the creation of public goods like safety and property rights as well as the fostering of an enabling environment for private action, be it in the area of business or civil society. Education, oriented towards inculcating civic values and a sense of belonging, is also seen as an area where the state exercises a critical role in socialising individuals to see themselves beyond their narrow parochial networks.

Based on the data here, it appears that the range of networks beyond immediate family to which ex-combatants have access is limited. This partly a reflection of the relative paucity of associational life in the areas surveyed. As with many (if not most) post-conflict societies, Angola seems to lack the requisite density of associational life that is generally found in thriving democracies. The question to ask then is whether these social networks are 'bonding' or 'bridging' in character.

Much social activity is still concentrated on the two major political parties – MPLA and UNITA – or around the churches. This is especially true in rural areas, where the single-party system is so deeply entrenched that even LIMA – seen as an 'opposition' women's group – may not be tolerated by the leaders of the MPLA women's group, OMA.[133] While membership of even a political organisation may help ex-combatants to bond to networks composed of other ex-combatants and people of similar background, this is 'bonding' as defined above: fundamentally exclusionary of others and with the effect of reinforcing political identities and diminishing broader and more socially beneficial ones. It is worrying – and indicative of this – that high levels of political organisational membership seem to be associated with lower levels of broader societal reintegration, leading to a greater probability of societal tension.

The other, in fact the principal, source of social networks comes from the church. Overall, this seems to be a 'bridging' network in this context. Ex-combatants, the research seems to indicate (although this should be followed up and verified with further research), are becoming integrated into churches and church social groups alongside other community members regardless of political affiliation. Ex-combatants report the positive messages of reconciliation that the church spreads within communities. And yet the churches can also form vertical networks. Interdenominational cooperation has been limited and fraught, and it is an accepted fact that a church will assist its own congregation in times of need – but only its own congregation. Churches thus follow the same pattern of exclusivity of association that political parties do, although the lines are drawn differently.

Social networks have played an important role, however, in ex-soldiers deciding where to settle. Extended family networks also seem to have a particular importance in facilitating the resettlement and reintegration of ex-combatants, in aspects including land access in rural areas, formal employment in urban areas, and the possibility of mobility between the two. Informal information networks communicate to ex-combatants the locations of their families across enormous distances, and pass messages as to whether and when resettlement may be possible. And traditional community leaders continue to exercise influence over their lives in times of trouble.

It would be a mistake to misread the paucity of membership in groups other than churches as a crippling deficiency in the building blocks of social capital. However, unfortunately, it would appear that the history of war and the constant search for security by Angolans has contributed to predominantly 'bonding' rather than 'bridging' networks – perhaps with the (partial) exception of the churches. Even families – seen to be so crucial in the reintegration process – are only partially trusted; this is perhaps not surprising given the political divisions that have split them in many cases (especially in the case of UNITA ex-combatants returning to formerly government-held areas). 'Friends' are generally limited to other ex-combatants and even then many ex-combatants in focus groups referred to the lack of real communication and discussion between them – for reasons of security.

The absence of bridging strategies will almost certainly constitute a major handicap for ex-combatants in their future options and development, since economic and other opportunities in Angola are largely dependent on access to informal networks. The predominance of exclusive, 'bonding' networks is also unlikely to assist in the breaking down of militarised identities. How this social foundation will affect the impulse towards political activism (as expressed by a sizable minority) will be important to the future of Angola's post-conflict settlement.

Reintegration and Political Participation

Political reintegration was seen by the project to be a cumulative 'bundle' of attitudes, beliefs and expectations with respect to the post-conflict political environment involving a commitment or, at the very least, willingness to participate in the democratic process. If identity and the formation of social capital are seen as fundamental to the functioning of a stable liberal democracy, then a willingness on the part of ex-soldiers to engage in political activity can be taken as a sign of rehabilitation and trust. As such, individuals were surveyed on the following:

- the degree to which ex-combatants hold attitudes and beliefs consonant with liberal democracy;

- the degree to which ex-combatants retain their conflict-era political affiliations;

- the sources of information on politics for ex-combatants which form the basis for choice;

- the degree to which ex-combatants are willing and feel they are able to participate in electoral activities.

When reviewing the data collected through the survey, a picture developed of the former UNITA combatant as knowledgeable about electoral politics, conscious of the democratic process in a most general way, cognisant of the opportunities that it presents but somewhat ambivalent about actively engaging in party politics itself. On this latter point, a significant number (54%) are keen to participate in electoral events, with a fifth of these willing to put themselves up as candidates for office. Concurrently, a strong streak of entitlement runs through the ex-combatants' approach to the post-conflict peace settlement in the sense that this group has considerable expectations of the government (expressed in terms of elections, jobs, training or land). The degree to which these expectations are met may also form part of the ex-combatants' long-term reintegration within Angolan society.

Liberal democratic values are primarily expressed through a commitment to elections and a belief that these will ensure peace. Perhaps surprisingly, a great deal of stock is placed in elections as laying the foundation for peace by the respondents. As Angola's history suggests, it is of crucial importance that this group sees any future elections as free and fair – though there is nothing in the project's findings (as mentioned above) that would imply a willingness on the part of the respondents to repeat UNITA's ill-fated reversion to civil war. The project did not survey for more generalised positions on liberal democracy, for example, attitudes towards majority-minority rule; the role of a constitution; and law in governing societal relations, etc. However, this material has been acquired by the International Republican Institute in Angola and, in a more general setting, through opinion surveys produced by the Afro-barometer.

For the ISS project, a willingness to participate in politics was seen to be both (1) a concrete expression of acceptance of the inefficacy of military means as an avenue for obtaining fundamental economic and political goods; and (2) faith in the ability of the post-conflict political system to accommodate the ex-combatants' concerns. That ex-combatants exhibited contrary positions on political participation is perhaps understandable given the proximity of war. What is more intriguing is that the project found that a majority was interested in participating in electoral politics and, furthermore, a significant minority (one fifth) would consider serving as candidates in an election.

This, of course, contradicts some of the earlier survey responses which are fairly emphatic in disavowing any interest in the proverbial 'meat and drink' of party politics, that is to say, organising meetings and campaigning for the party. Even if one accounts for this interest as recognition of the convergence between access to economic goods and the holding of political office, it is telling that over a hundred people have sufficient faith in the functionality of electoral politics to put themselves up for office.

Here it is important to give consideration to the evolving powers of local authorities, especially over budgets, but within the framework of some form of public scrutiny that prevents against the worst forms of abuses of office. Faith in democracy – the kind that ultimately gives rise to a sustained commitment to electoral politics – is rooted in its experience locally and there is a need to ensure that elected officials have the means with which to demonstrate positive change for the constituencies that gave them their support.

A crucial dimension of democratic practice is access to an independent media. Knowledge of political parties, or rather the absence of that knowledge in the case of most of the individuals surveyed, is linked to the media as the primary – though not exclusive, especially in a 'traditionalist' society – source of information within the wider community. The bias of the state-run media in Angola has been the subject of criticism by both UNITA and outside observers for many years. What this survey seems to suggest is that the newer political parties will remain outside of the public imagination as long as the media is dominated by the state. Again, survey work done by Afro-barometer corroborates the levels of support for democracy with the openness of its media, with Zimbabwe scoring the lowest of 16 African countries surveyed (Afro-barometer 2004). However, despite criticism of state-run media, there is no discernable anti-democratic bias detected amongst those who listen to it versus those who tune into international radio stations.

It is worth noting that the economic standing of former combatants is suggestive of interesting, if somewhat contradictory, findings in assessing it as a guide to levels of political participation. For example, the rates of membership of political organisations are highest amongst the landless and those who lease land, something that hints at the possibility of future political action around the land issue. Political activism, following from this data, is seen as an instrument for improving economic opportunities (and as such fully in concert with established democratic practice). More generally, if one considers the broader levels of interest in participation in politics, it would appear that while a majority of ex-soldiers may not be inclined to political activism a sizable minority see it as an option if not an opportunity. Clues as to how this activism will be manifest remain elusive but, based on the survey data (beyond the associations of the past with UNITA), none of the political parties has any particular command over this group at this stage.

Reintegration and Sustainable Livelihoods

> The domestic economy is composed of four main agents as follows: the state, interventionist and all-powerful, an economy which acts as the Foreign Bank of the country, the ever growing informal economy and a formal economy with no support from the state and that is late in becoming the most important economic actor in the country...if we add to this the fact that this economy is practically all located in a narrow coastal area of the country, then one realises the important structural deficiencies existent in Angola.[134]

> In the re-launching of production and the re-establishment of social services to rural communities, the family unit must be the programme's reference point...it represents the 'productive cell' of rural communities – it can be thought of as a family based rural enterprise, simultaneously a unit of production and a unit of consumption, characterised by the fact that the whole family works towards its productive activities'.[135]

As discussed above, there is no doubt that factors of an economic nature (access to land, jobs, training but also housing and basic services) are determinants of the successful reintegration of former combatants and all other vulnerable groups. Yet it would be unrealistic to think about livelihoods of vulnerable populations in isolation from the context of the country as a whole. Although it is often referred to in the literature on reintegration, the importance of the broader economic and institutional environment is often forgotten during the design of reintegration programmes and strategies. As correctly noted by the GTZ,

> ...in many cases, the efforts to support demobilisation and reintegration lack sufficient links with the broader post-war rehabilitation, capacity-building, and general development strategies, policies and programmes.[136]

Angola's population of an estimated at 13 million grows at an average of 2,9% a year. As with other countries in the region, Angola has a growing and progressively urbanised, young population actively looking for employment – in fact, it is estimated that every year the country has roughly 300,000 young people looking for their first job.

Unemployment is rife in the country, with an average of 35% unemployment in the main urban areas of Luanda, Cabinda, Benguela, Moxico and Huíla according to the National Statistics Institute. Expectations of formal employment are generally low, especially for those without formal qualifications. The vast majority of Angolans survive through occasional labour in the informal economy, which guarantees the livelihood of a considerable and increasingly growing number of families in the urban and peri-urban areas – a pattern uncovered by this project as regards former combatants and by other projects as regards other vulnerable groups.[137]

Economic reintegration and the restoration of sustainable livelihoods at local, household and individual level are inextricably linked with the diversification of sources of income through the (re)creation of productive and domestic assets. In turn, these depend on the rehabilitation of infrastructure and the extension and strengthening of state administration at all levels but particularly at local level, where the provision of basic services is, at best deficient, at worst inexistent.[138] All of these require the stabilisation of the macro-economic situation in the country, for which the revitalisation of the national economy (strengthening the business sector both public and private) is extremely important, as is financial stability.

For all the above, professional/technical training (in areas as diverse as agriculture or business skills) together with formal education are critical for the future development of the country – a need recognised in no uncertain terms by Angola's National Assembly (*Lei de Base do Sistema Nacional de Formação Profissional*). Yet, these require a developmental vision, one that places the most vulnerable at its centre, one geared towards poverty alleviation while grounded in a sound national economic recovery plan. For all the good intentions of a number of training programmes that were implemented in the immediate resettlement phase, if they are developed in isolation of such a vision, the probability of equipping the former combatant with the skills needed for a sustainable livelihood is extremely low.

In Bié province, the project had some evidence of the lack of efficacy of professional training programmes that are geared towards former combatants but largely developed in isolation of the broader post-war rehabilitation and general development strategies. This was particular the case for the poverty reduction strategy process that was underway at the time of the project. During 2003, a team from INEFOP (National Institute for Employment and Professional Training) began a training programme for former combatants in Andulo – by the time the project had arrived the team had already completed three training cycles in the municipality and 422 former combatants had received training in skills relevant to the reconstruction effort (as electricians, builders, carpenters, and plumbers).

Although the INEFOP team was very enthusiastic and dedicated to its mission (encapsulated by the programme's title 'We're With You', or "*Estamos Contigo*"), it faced considerable challenges. The training of 422 individuals out of a population of around 20,000 (in Andulo municipality alone) gives some idea of the limitations. Needless to say, a severe scarcity of resources limited the real impact of such programmes. For example, very few learners received the kits needed to start their new professions. However, what was perhaps the greatest limitation of all was the lack of follow-up to the training by municipal or provincial administrations, which could have either incorporated or, at the very least, provided advice to this new, available 'workforce'.[139]

This lack of capacity in the majority of municipalities has been often recognised by the government and its international partners. As detailed in chapter 2, in each area surveyed, problems of an institutional nature have included the fragility of structures meant to support communities; the absence of mechanisms for the control and follow-up of projects and programmes, including with NGOs and other organisations; or the deficient provision of all basic services, but particularly primary health care and education. In Bié, more than two years after the war's end, lack of institutional capacity remained a serious obstacle to the adequate support of reintegration programmes.

It should be noted that resolving Angola's lack of administrative capacity and extension of state administration is a mammoth task which will take many years. Yet, this recognition alone could have given a different direction to efforts such as those by the INEFOP. A 'working hypothesis' in this regard relates to the strengthening of the organisational capacity of former combatants and other vulnerable groups "from below". An interesting example was given to the project in Kuíto – in order to rehabilitate the bridge at Cutaco, a group of former combatants decided to form a group comprising several individuals with the expertise needed. Yet, even though they presented their project to the local administration, they were never called upon.

Will Angola, with its vast and untapped natural resources, have the capacity to undertake all of the above while maintaining social stability by 'managing' the high level of expectations of all population groups? Will the country successfully navigate the transition towards a 'real' (nationwide) market economy and away from an 'enclave economy' strongly dependent on oil? As one moves from the national to the local and individual levels, the linkages between them, from a policy implementation perspective, seem to disappear. It is not surprising that development actors in the country have pushed for poverty reduction strategies based on a permanent dialogue between the national and the local level. In fact, the current impoverishment of Angolans is not attributed to the absence of economic growth but to a 'substantial worsening of the conditions of distribution of national income'. In addition, as pointed out by *Universidade Católica*, this is a concrete case of economic growth deepening under-development: 'if the assumptions that currently underlie the distribution of income from oil are not substantially altered, the perverse effects of the oil economy on the Angolan economy and society will increase'.[140]

ENDNOTES

1   Reverend Daniel Ntoni-Nzinga, a Baptist minister and respected church leader, in an interview to Ofeibea Quist-Arcton of AllAfrica.com on 21 June 2005. See < http://allafrica.com/stories/200206210195.html>.

2   DD&R programmes have in recent years become part of official development policy of a number of agencies, including the OECD (1997), the United Nations Department of Peacekeeping Operations, amongst others. See in this regard B Eisenblatter and B Hoffmann, 'Preface' in *Demobilisation and Reintegration of Ex-combatants in Post-War and Transition Countries: Trends and Challenges of External Support*, GTZ, Division 43: Health, Education, Nutrition and Emergency Aid, 2001.

3   For an overview of previous DD&R processes in Angola, see J Gomes Porto and Imogen Parsons, *Sustaining the Peace in Angola: An overview of current demobilisation, disarmament and reintegration*, Monograph 83, Pretoria, ISS, April 2003, pp 19-30.

4   The 'Memorandum of Understanding for the Cessation of Hostilities and the Resolution of the Outstanding Military Issues under the Lusaka Protocol' signed on 4 April 2002.

5   Gomes Porto and Parsons, op cit, p 31.

6   United Nations, *Angola: The post-war challenges*, Common Country Assessment, New York, 2002, p 51.

7   Office for the Coordination of Humanitarian Affairs in Angola (OCHA), *Humanitarian Update*, 2002-2004.

8   Gomes Porto and Parsons, op cit, p 9.

9   OCHA, *Humanitarian Update*, op cit. Based on information from MINARS (UTCAH), Government of Angola.

10 Gomes Porto and Parsons, op cit, p 32.

11 Ibid, p 33. Data based on press statements by the Joint Military Commission.

12 For a working set of definitions of DD&R phases, see N de Watteville, *Addressing gender issues in demobilisation and reintegration programmes*, Africa Region Working Paper Series, World Bank, 2002, p 6.

13   World Bank, *Aide Memoire: Angola Demobilisation and Reintegration Programme*, Luanda, 16 August 2002.

14   Gomes Porto and Parsons, op cit, p 35.

15   World Bank, *Aide Memoire: Project Implementation Support Mission, Angola Demobilisation and Reintegration Programme*, Luanda, 28 February 2004. The report notes that 'this number represents 1,116 more ex-combatants than are confirmed by the FAA, which IRSEM attributes to double registrations at provincial offices that will be cleared up when the information is recorded in IRSEM's database.'

16   Ministério da Assistência e Reinserção Social, Unidade Técnica de Coordenação da Ajuda Humanitária (UTCAH), *Síntese sobre a situação humanitária em Angola, Abril/Junho 2004*, Luanda, 20 August 2004.

17   See GTZ, *Demobilisation and Reintegration of Ex-combatants in Post-War and Transition Countries: Trends and Challenges of External Support*, GTZ, Division 43: Health, Education, Nutrition and Emergency Aid, 2001. A number of relevant policy papers have informed this gradual shift, *inter alia*: United Nations, *The Causes of Conflict and the Promotion of Peace and Sustainable Development in Africa*, Report of the UN Secretary-General, A/52/871 – S/1998/3/318, New York, 1998; the OECD/DAC, *Conflict, Peace and Development Co-operation on the threshold of the 21st century*, Development Co-operation Guidelines Series, Paris, 1998; United Nations, *Disarmament, Demobilisation and Reintegration of Ex-combatants in a Peacekeeping Environment*, Lessons Learned Unit of the UN Department of Peacekeeping Operations, New York, 1999; and United Nations, *The Role of United Nations Peacekeeping in Disarmament, Demobilisation and Reintegration*, Report of the Secretary General to the Security Council, S/2000/101, 11 February 2000.

18   GTZ, *Demobilisation and Reintegration of Ex-combatants in Post-War and Transition Countries: Trends and Challenges of External Support*, GTZ, Division 43: Health, Education, Nutrition and Emergency Aid, 2001, p 7.

19   United Nations, Department of Peacekeeping Operations, Cartographic Section, Map No. 3727 Rev. 3 January 2004. < http://www.un.org/Depts/Cartographic/map/profile/angola.pdf>.

20   See in this regard O Monteiro e A Caetano de Sousa, Descentralização em Angola, in *A Descentralização em Angola, Programa das Nações Unidas para o Desenvolvimento* (PNUD), March 2002, p 75.

21   In addition to issues around the constitutionally defined role of representing the state in the areas of justice, finance and interior at local level, it is interesting to note the structure of municipal and communal administrations because they represent (where they have been implemented) the most immediate face

of the state for the majority of people. Municipal administrations relate to provincial governments through the GACAMC (Gabinete de Apoio e Controlo das Administracoes Municipais e Comunais). Composed of one administrator and a deputy administrator, municipal administrations are meant to include a municipal council as well as perform a variety of administrative functions – including planning, research, social and community services as well as economic coordination in the municipality.

22 According to data provided by the representative of the Institute for Socio-Professional Reintegration of Ex-Military Personnel (IRSEM) during the project's interim workshop in Johannesburg on 13 and 14 September 2004.

23 Data provided at the project's workshop in Johannesburg, September 2004.

24 In fact, all areas surveyed in this project are part of Agricultural Zone VII as defined in the government's strategy for support to social reinsertion. Ministério da Assistencia e Reinserção Social/Banco Mundial-IDA, *Operacionalização da Estratégia de Apoio a Reinserção Social (volume 1, Programa)*, Projecto de Reabilitação Social Pós-Conflicto (PRSPC), Luanda, November 2002.

25 Provincial Group for the Assessment of Vulnerability. In Huambo, the members of this group include ADRA-A; ADRA-I; ASA; CIC; CONCERN; DW; FAO; GACAMC; IMC; IRSEM; MEDICOS DO MUNDO; MINADER; MINARS; MINSA; MSF-F; MOVIMONDO; OADECO; OCHA; OIKOS; OMS; Oxfam; PAM; SC-UK; SOLIDARITES; Unicef; UTCAH; UNSECOOR and World Vision.

26 Republica de Angola, *Huambo: Perfil Socioeconómico*, April 2003.

27 Província do Huambo, Grupo Provincial de Avaliação da Vulnerabilidade, *Avaliação da Vulnerabilidade da População à Insegurança Alimentar Novembro/03 a Abril/04*, Huambo, May 2004.

28 United Nations, OCHA.

29 Província do Huambo, op cit, p 5.

30 Ibid, p 4.

31 Ibid, p 9.

32 Republica de Angola, *Huambo: Perfil Socioeconómico*, April 2003. Translation by the authors.

33 Education; Health; Assistance and Social Reintegration – Former Combatants and War Veterans; Agriculture and Rural Development, Fisheries and Environment; Trade, Industry and Tourism; Public Administration, Employment and Social Security; Energy and Water; Youth and Sport; Public Works, Urbanisation and Housing; Media; Transport and Communications; and, finally, Family and Promotion of Women.

34 Republica de Angola, op cit, p 18.

35   Ibid, p 15.

36   The province has 6,422 teachers, including those teaching in high schools and adult learning centres. 39% of the teachers are in rural areas.

37   Republica de Angola, op cit, p 16.

38   Ibid, p 16.

39   Ibid, p 21.

40   Although informal estimates put it as low as a quarter to a third of a million, the estimate of between 750,000 and 800,000 was provided by the UN's OCHA in Huambo; while the estimate of 903,375 was provided by the Provincial Group for the Assessment of Vulnerability in Huambo.

41   For a detailed description of the various government agencies that deal with reintegration of former combatants in Angola see Gomes Porto and Parsons, op cit, pp 19-30.

42   Província do Huambo, Grupo Provincial de Avaliação da Vulnerabilidade, Avaliação da Vulnerabilidade da População à Insegurança Alimentar Novembro/03 a Abril/04, Huambo, May 2004, p 8.

43   Data from OCHA.

44   Interview, IRSEM, Tchicala Tcholoanga, January 2004.

45   See Província do Bié, Grupo Provincial de Análise da Vulnerabilidade, Avaliação da Vulnerabilidade da População à Insegurança Alimentar Novembro/03 a Abril/04, Bié, May 2004. In Bié, the members of this group include AFRICARE; CARE; CONCERN; CVA; CVE; FSCA; GABINETE DO PLANO; HALO TRUST; MINADER/IDA; MINARS; MINSA; MOVIMONDO; MSF-B; OCHA; OMS; PAM; UNICEF and UTCAH.

46   Republica de Angola, *Perfil Provincial do Bié*, April 2003, p 17. Translation by the authors.

47   Ministério da Assistencia e Reinserção Social/Banco Mundial-IDA, *Operacionalização da Estratégia de Apoio a Reinserção Social (volume 2, Documentos de Apoio)*, Projecto de Reabilitação Social Pós-Conflicto (PRSPC), Luanda, November 2002.

48   See in this regard Republica de Angola, *Perfil Provincial do Bié*, April 2003, p 6. Translation by the authors.

49   Ibid, p 2.

50   Província do Bié, Grupo Provincial de Análise da Vulnerabilidade, Avaliação da Vulnerabilidade da População à Insegurança Alimentar Novembro/03 a Abril/04, Bié, May 2004.

51   These are responsible for education; health; assistance and social reintegration
      – including former combatants and war veterans; agriculture and rural
      development, fisheries and the environment; trade, industry and tourism;
      public administration, employment and social security; energy and water;
      youth and sport; public works, urbanisation and housing; media; transport and
      communications; and, finally, family and promotion of women.

52   Republica de Angola, *Perfil Provincial do Bié*, April 2003. Translation by the
      authors.

53   Ibid, p 13.

54   Ibid.

55   Ibid, p 23.

56   Ibid.

57   In fact, the government has identified a number of obstacles to the proper
      functioning of health programmes in the province: (1) difficult access to
      municipalities and communes; as a result of destroyed roads and mines; (2)
      absence of proper means of transport to reach more remote areas; (3) insufficient
      and irregularly supplied drugs and medication; (4) severe lack of material,
      financial and human resources' means and finally, absence of adequate means
      of communication within the province.

58   Republica de Angola, *Perfil Provincial do Bié*, April 2003, p 3. Translation by the
      authors.

59   Interview, Médecins sans Frontières (MSF – Spain), Kuíto, February 2004.

60   Província do Bié, Grupo Provincial de Análise da Vulnerabilidade, Avaliação
      da Vulnerabilidade da População à Insegurança Alimentar Novembro/03 a
      Abril/04, Bié, May 2004.

61   The market of Chissindo, just outside Kuito town, is a good example of this
      – everything from food items to electrical appliances, from Chinese-made
      motorcycles to live cattle can be purchased here.

62   When the war ended, WFP initiated the provision of emergency assistance
      to the families of former combatants in 'family reception areas'. During the
      resettlement/return process, the agency decided to treat all populations in the
      same way, including former combatants, now demobilised. The idea behind this
      was that WFP did not want to contribute to differentiation or competition for
      scarce resources at the local level. Interview, World Food Programme Office,
      Kuíto, February 2004.

63   Província do Bié, Grupo Provincial de Análise da Vulnerabilidade, Avaliação
      da Vulnerabilidade da População à Insegurança Alimentar Novembro/03 a
      Abril/04, Bié, May 2004.

64   Termed 'regiões de recuperação agro-mercantil'. See in this regard, Grupo Provincial de Análise de Vulnerabilidade, 'Avaliação da Vulnerabilidade da População a Insegurança Alimentar', May 2003 to October 2003.

65   Província do Bié, op cit, p 7.

66   Interview, International Committee of the Red Cross (Genéve), Office in Kuíto, February 2004.

67   Província do Bié, op cit, p 7.

68   Ibid, p 13.

69   Governo Provincial do Bié, Direcção Provincial da Agricultura, Desenvolvimento Rural, Pescas e Ambiente.

70   Republica de Angola, *Perfil Provincial do Bié*, April 2003, p 35. Translation by the authors.

71   Ibid, p 16.

72   Ibid, p 15.

73   Provincial Commission for the Social and Productive Reintegration of the Demobilised and Displaced.

74   To confuse matters further, UNITA's Municipal Secretary in Andulo claims there are 24,000 former combatants in the municipality alone, while the Deputy Administrator of Andulo (a former UNITA military) says that only 18,000 former combatants are in the municipality.

75   So as to minimise bias, former combatants were informed that no payment would be provided for the interviews (either in cash or kind).

76   Adapted from WFP, data from 'Gabinete de Apoio às Administrações Municipais/ Governo Provincial', MINSA, OMS, UNICEF, MINARS and IRSEM.

77   Approximately 1,479,240 urban and 1,533,381 rural according to the Provincial Government's Statistics Department. See also Republica de Angola, *Huíla – Perfil Sócio-Económico*, Abril 2003, p 4.

78   Ibid, p 13.

79   The strengthening and development of adequate functional links between the provincial and municipal administrations, as well as the need for training and placement of additional staff at both levels, was also highlighted in the province's socio-economic profile. Ibid, p 14.

80   Ibid.

81   Republica de Angola, *Huíla – Perfil Sócio-Económico*, Abril 2003, p 18.

82   Ibid.

83 Republica de Angola, *Huíla – Perfil Sócio-Económico*, Abril 2003, p 13.

84 We should note the potential role in terms of rural development strategies that can be played by the Rural Development Stations (EDAS – Estações de Desenvolvimento Agrário) of which the ones in Lubango, Humpata and Quipungo had been rehabilitated at the time of the research. Ibid, p 31.

85 Ibid, p 32.

86 Província da Huíla, Grupo Provincial de Análise da Vulnerabilidade, *Avaliação da Vulnerabilidade da População à Insegurança Alimentar Novembro/03 a Abril/04*, Lubango, May 2004.

87 For example, the Associação Agro-Pecuária Comercial e Industrial da Huíla (APCIL), the Associação das mulheres empresárias da Huíla (AMEH) and the União Nacional de Apoio as Associações de Camponeses (UNACA). In this regard, see Republica de Angola, *Huila – Perfil Socio-Economico*, Abril 2003, p 16.

88 Ibid, p 32.

89 A technical college focused on agriculture is based in Humpata, the Instituto Médio Agrário do Tchivinguiro.

90 Republica de Angola, *Huíla – Perfil Sócio-Económico*, Abril 2003, p 32.

91 Ibid.

92 Ibid, p 14-15.

93 Information provided by the Joint Military Commission (JMC) during July 2002. By May 2003, 10,000 people were still waiting to be transported from gathering areas; 400 were living in two transit centres in Lubango; 1,000 people were living in a reception area in Chicomba, with a further 1,200 people living in an abandoned school, a hospital and in temporary shelters in Chipindo.

94 Republica de Angola, *Huila – Perfil Socio-Economico*, Abril 2003.

95 Interviews conducted *in situ* by J Gomes Porto, June 2002.

96 Approximately 45% in Angola's main urban centres.

97 N de Watteville, *Addressing gender issues in demobilisation and reintegration programmes*, Africa Region Working Paper Series, World Bank, 2002, p 6.

98 I Nübler, 'Human resources development and utilization in demobilization and reintegration programs, Bonn International Center for Conversion, Paper 7, January 1997, p 3.

99 N de Watteville, op cit, p 12.

100 Província do Bié, Grupo Provincial de Análise da Vulnerabilidade, *Avaliação da Vulnerabilidade da População à Insegurança Alimentar: Novembro 2003 a Abril 2004*, Kuíto, May 2004, p 7.

101 Ibid.

102 As is the perennial question of the real autonomy of the *Soba* from local level government influences in those cases where they receive subsidies from local government, and/or are identified with the ruling the party, the MPLA.

103 See *inter alia* Gomes Porto and Parsons, op cit.

104 See for example *Background Paper Drafted as preparation for the ECHA Working Group Paper, "Harnessing Institutional Capacities in support of DDR of Former Combatants"*, Praxis Group Ltd, 6 June 2000.

105 Kees Kingma, "Post-War Demobilisation, Reintegration and Peace-Building," *paper presented at the* International Conference and Expert Group Meeting on 'The Contribution of Disarmament and Conversion to Conflict Prevention and its Relevance for Development Cooperation', Bonn, 30-31 August 1999.

106 Although a multitude of factors explain the breakdown of the two previous peace processes, the depth of distrust and suspicion that has historically characterised the relationship between the two belligerents is fundamental to an understanding of the intractability of Angola's civil war. In fact, with the collapse of each peace process, the level of suspicion and distrust increased exponentially, entrenching both parties in rigid positions, deepening their mutual hostility and feeding their perceptions of the other as a dishonest and untrustworthy adversary, ultimately bent on total annihilation. And the end of war in Angola did come about through military victory of one side over the other and not through the voluntary attendance of the parties at the negotiation table.

107 Interview by J Gomes Porto, Luanda, 2002.

108 International Republican Institute, *Percepções dos Angolanos em relação às próximas eleições'*, IPES/IRR Luanda, July 2004.

109 Praxis Group, *Background Paper drafted in preparation for the ECHA Working Group Paper 'Harnessing Institutional Capacities in Support of DDR of Former Combatants,'* 6 June 2000.

110 International Republican Institute, op cit.

111 However, this does not seem to correlate with ex-combatants' identity perceptions of themselves – although the overall dataset does correlate. For some, as yet inexplicable reason, the correlation holds in Huambo Province & Bie (less strongly), but not in Huila.

112 Again, a parallel with the survey produced by IRI may be highlighted. On the issue of 'willingness to work in the next elections as part of a campaign', the survey found that the majority lived in a peri-urban area (67.4%).

113 GTZ, *Demobilisation and Reintegration of Ex-combatants in Post-War and Transition Countries: Trends and Challenges of External Support,* GTZ, Division 43: Health, Education, Nutrition and Emergency Aid, 2001.

114 International Republican Institute, op cit.

115 'Classic analysis' of social capital include R Putnam, *Making Democracy Work*, Princeton, NJ: Princeton University Press, 1993; J Coleman, Social capital in the creation of human capital, *American Journal of Sociology*, 94, 1988, ppp 95–120 and F Fukuyama, Social capital and the global economy, *Foreign Affairs*, 74 (5), ppp 89–103, 1995. See also the excellent critique by Frans J Schuurman, Social Capital: the politico-emancipatory potential of a disputed concept, *Third World Quarterly*, Vol 24, No 6, 2003, ppp 991–1010.

116 As noted by Schuurman, 'in an enlightening contribution to the 2000 Exeter conference on social capital, Pippa Norris (2000) emphasised the difference between social capital and trust. Using data from the World Values Study surveys and the UNDP Human Development Index, she noted that 'Social capital is associated with socioeconomic development...but this link appears to operate through social trust not civic society' (Norris, 2000: 12). According to Norris's findings, Putnam is 'at least half right' in the sense that, of the two components of social capital, it is primarily social trust and not associational networks that seems the most active component related to democratic development'. F J Schuurman, Social Capital: the politico-emancipatory potential of a disputed concept, *Third World Quarterly*, Vol 24, No 6, p 1001, 2003.

117 Central to this may be the fact that birthright in particular is a central part of customary law, which still largely dictates land access and inheritance in rural Angola but is being overtaken by other more commercial factors in and around urban areas. It is thus more difficult for an 'outsider' to resettle in a rural area than an urban one, and to acquire the land and goods necessary for an effective resettlement and reintegration.

118 Witness the following proposition put forward by GTZ: '*failure to adequately address the risks involved in demobilisation may jeopardise sustainable peace-building and human development. Without support, demobilised soldiers and guerrilla fighters might have great difficulties in re-establishing themselves in civilian life, and frustrated ex-combatants may threaten the peace and development process by becoming involved in criminal activities or violent political opposition'*. GTZ, *Demobilisation and Reintegration of Ex-combatants in Post-War and Transition Countries: Trends and Challenges of External Support*, GTZ, Division 43: Health, Education, Nutrition and Emergency Aid, 2001.

119 Kees Kingma, "Post-War Demobilisation, Reintegration and Peace-building," *paper presented at the* International Conference and Expert-Group Meeting on "The contribution of disarmament and conversion to conflict prevention and its relevance for development cooperation", Bonn, 30-31 August 1999, pp 10-11. For a more detailed discussion of this issue see also GTZ, *Demobilisation and Reintegration of Ex-combatants in Post-War and Transition Countries: Trends and Challenges of External Support*, GTZ, Division 43: Health, Education, Nutrition and Emergency Aid, 2001.

120   As noted by GTZ *'demobilisation, disarmament, resettlement and reintegration are all complex processes particularly after the end of a violent conflict, and they are politically sensitive...[they] take place within a distinct political and socio-economic context. They usually involve a large number of different actors, each with their particular roles and interests'*. GTZ, op cit, p 12.

121   As noted, an exception to the rule concerned those who were trained in 'public sector' jobs (as teachers, nurses, etc) which corresponded, as discussed above, to 14.9% of the total.

122   Although, as noted above, the average size of the former combatants' household is larger than that of the national average (with an average of 9 versus the national average of 5.1 s for Angola's rural areas). See WFP, *Angola: Vulnerability Assessment in Rural Areas - National Overview,* Vulnerability Analysis and Food Aid Working Group Chaired by WFP/VAM Unit, Luanda, June 2004.

123   We should nevertheless point out that these statistics apply to rural Angola and therefore any comparisons must be done cautiously – we have included them because they provide additional clues as to the vulnerability profiles of groups other than former combatants. See WFP, *Angola: Vulnerability Assessment in Rural Areas - National Overview,* Vulnerability Analysis and Food Aid Working Group Chaired by WFP/VAM Unit, Luanda, June 2004, p 8.

124   Ibid.

125   Ibid.

126   Ibid.

127   This very point was noted by Kingma in the following terms: "the official termination of the armed conflict usually brings high expectations. After much suffering, a new peaceful life full of opportunities is to begin...if the expectations of being able to set up an independent sustainable livelihood are not directly met, this causes frustration". Kees Kingma, "Post-War Demobilisation, Reintegration and Peace-building," International Conference and Expert-Group Meeting on "The contribution of disarmament and conversion to conflict prevention and its relevance for development cooperation", Bonn, 30-31 August 1999, p 6.

128   Background Paper drafted as preparation for the ECHA Working Group Paper, *"Harnessing Institutional Capacities in support of DDR of Former Combatants",* Praxis Group Ltd, 6 June 2000, p 1.

129   As noted by the World Bank, "a key component of achieving the transition from war to peace relates to the successful social and economic reintegration of war-affected populations. These populations include not only repatriated refugees and ex-combatants but also internally displaced peoples and populations affected by conflict whose social and economic systems have been destroyed as a result of the conflict". World Bank, *Re-integration of War Affected Populations – The Transition from War to Peace: An Overview.*

130 It constitutes the cultural component of modern societies, which in other respects have been organised since the Enlightenment on the basis of formal institutions, the rule of law, and rationality. Building social capital has typically been seen as a task for "second generation" economic reform; but unlike economic policies or even economic institutions, social capital cannot be so easily created or shaped by public policy.' See F Fukuyama, Social capital and the global economy, *Foreign Affairs*, 74 (5), pp 89–103, 1995.

131 R Putnam, *Making Democracy Work*, Princeton, NJ: Princeton University Press, 1993.

132 Oddly enough, there is little mention in the literature on social capital of the difficulties that extra-societal entities, be they donor countries, multilateral agencies and private foundations presumably encounter in this area.

133 This attitude was found by researchers in one rural village in Huambo province.

134 Universidade Católica de Angola, *Relatório Económico de Angola 2002*, Centro de Estudos e Investigação Científica, October 2003, p 4.

135 Ministério da Assistencia e Reinserção Social/Banco Mundial-IDA, *Operacionalização da Estratégia de Apoio a Reinserção Social* (volume 1, Programa), Projecto de Reabilitação Social Pós-Conflicto (PRSPC), Luanda, November 2002, p 23. Translation by the authors.

136 GTZ, *Demobilisation and Reintegration of Ex-combatants in Post-War and Transition Countries: Trends and Challenges of External Support*, GTZ, Division 43: Health, Education, Nutrition and Emergency Aid, 2001, p 15.

137 Ministério da Assistencia e Reinserção Social/Banco Mundial-IDA, *Operacionalização da Estratégia de Apoio a Reinserção Social (volume 1, Programa)*, Projecto de Reabilitação Social Pós-Conflicto (PRSPC), Luanda, November 2002, p 6. Translation by the authors.

138 One of the most interesting findings of this project was that, by and large, former combatants regarded the traditional authority (*Soba*) as the most important person in the community and the one to turn to in case of problems. It would be interesting to find out what other vulnerable groups' responses would be as an indicator of the perception that communities have of local administration.

139 A similar situation was highlighted by a group of low-ranking officers in Mitcha commune in Lubango (Huíla) who referred to the short duration of the training courses and the fact that they were not in a condition to apply their new skills due to a lack of proper activity kits. In Lubango, for example, INEFOP only trained 125 former combatants and that training was considered inadequate.

140 Universidade Católica de Angola, op cit, p 5.

BIBLIOGRAPHY

C Alden, "Lessons from the Reintegration of Demobilised Soldiers in Mozambique," *Security Dialogue,* 33 (3), September 2002.

N Ball, *Complex crisis and complex peace: humanitarian coordination in Angola,* United Nations Office for the Coordination of Humanitarian Affairs. OCHA Online. <www.reliefweb.int/ocha_ol/pub/angola/>.

M Berdal, "Disarmament and demobilisation after civil war," International Institute for Strategic Studies, *Adelphi Paper,* 303, 1996.

Care International Angola, *Land & Natural Resource Management System Assessment, Bie Province, Angola,* Care International Angola, March 2004.

J S Coleman, "*Social Capital in the Creation of Human Capital,*" *American Journal of Sociology,* 94, 1988.

Comissão Intersectorial para o Processo de Paz e Reconciliação Nacional (Comité Executivo), *Programa de Reintegração Social dos Desmobilizados dos Ex-Militares da UNITA,* Abril 2002.

Commissão Provincial de Reintegração Social e Produtiva dos Desmobilizados e Deslocados, *Mapa de Controlo dos Desmobilizados e Deslocados do Memorandum do Luena,* Bicesse e Lusaka, Governo da Província do Bié, 30 September 2003.

Conselho de Ministros, "Decreto No1/01, Normas sobre o Reassentamento das Populacoes Deslocadas," *Diario da Republica,* Sexta-Feira, 5 de Janeiro de 2001.

Development Workshop, *Land and Reintegration of Ex-Combatants in Huambo Province in Post-War Angola,* Luanda, April 2004.

Development Workshop/Centre for Common Ground, *Action Research on Priorities for Peace-building in Angola: Huambo Province Pilot Research December 2002–March 2003,* Luanda, July 2003.

DFID, *Programme and technical assistance to Angola disarmament demobilisation and reintegration process,* August 2002- September 2002, 30 September 2002.

F S Schuurman, "*Social Capital: the politico-emancipatory potential of a disputed concept,*" *Third World Quarterly,* Vol 24, No 6, 2003.

F Fukuyama, *Social Capital and Civil Society*, paper presented at the Institute of Public Policy, George Mason University, 1 October 1999.

J Gomes Porto and I Parsons, *Sustaining the Peace in Angola. An Overview of Current Demobilisation, Disarmament and Reintegration*. Bonn International Centre for Conversion (BICC), Paper 27, March 2003. Also published by the Institute for Security Studies, Monograph Series, No. 83, April 2003.

J Gomes Porto, 'Angola at DD+040: Preliminary Assessment of the quartering, disarmament and demobilisation process.' *African Security Analysis Programme Situation Report*, 4 June 2002. <www.issafrica.org>

J Gomes Porto, 'Angola Quarterly Risk Assessment: January to February 2004' in *FAST Update*, SwissPeace, Swiss Agency for Development and Cooperation, March 2004.

J Gomes Porto, 'Contemporary Conflict Analysis in Perspective'. *Scarcity and Surfeit: The Ecology of Africa's Conflicts'*, Jeremy Lind and Kathryn Sturman (Eds), Institute for Security Studies, June, 2002.

Governo da Província do Bié, *Mapa Demográfico por faixas etárias da população a nivel da Província*, Gabinete de Apoio e Controlo das Administrações Municipais e Comunais, 12 December 2003.

Governo de Unidade e Reconciliação Nacional, *Projecto Cidadania Emprego, Estamos Contigo*, MAPESS, 7 November 2002.

GTZ, *Demobilisation and Reintegration of Ex-Combatants in Post-War and Transition Countries: Trends and Challenges of External Support*, GTZ, Division 43: Health, Education, Nutrition and Emergency Aid, 2001.

Human Rights Watch, *Struggling Through Peace: Return and Resettlement in Angola*, Vol. 15, No. 16 (A), Washington D.C., August 2003.

S Huntington and J Nelson, *No Easy Choice: political participation in developing countries*, Cambridge, MA: Harvard UP 1976.

Instituto de Reintegração Sócio Profissional dos Ex-Militares, *Programa Geral de Desmobilização e Reintegração*, IRSEM Central, May 2003.

International Crisis Group, "Angola's Choice: Reform or Regress," *Africa Report*, No. 61, Luanda/Brussels, 7 April 2003.

International Crisis Group, "Dealing With Savimbi's Ghost: The Security and Humanitarian Challenges in Angola," *Africa Report*, No. 58, Luanda/Brussels, 26 February 2003.

International Organisation for Migration, *UNITA ex-FMU soldiers demographic, socio-economic profiles for return and reintegration planning activities*, Geneva, October 2002.

International Republican Institute, *Percepções dos Angolanos em relação às próximas eleições*, IPES/IRR Luanda, July 2004.

K Kingma, "Post-War Demobilisation, Reintegration and Peace-building," International Conference and Expert-Group Meeting on "The contribution of disarmament and conversion to conflict prevention and its relevance for development cooperation", Bonn, 30-31 August 1999.

A Lari, "Returning home to a normal life? The plight of Angola's internally displaced," *African Security Analysis Programme Occasional Paper*, 5 February 2004.

Memorandum of Understanding Addendum to the Lusaka Protocol for the Cessation of Hostilities and the Resolution of the Outstanding Military Issues under the Lusaka Protocol, April 2004.

Ministério da Assistencia e Reinserção Social, Instituto de Reintegração Sócio-Profissional dos Ex-Militares. *Programa geral de desmobilização e reintegração*, 10 de Outubro de 2002.

Ministério da Assistencia e Reinserção Social/Banco Mundial-IDA, *Operacionalização da Estratégia de Apoio a Reinserção Social (volume 1, Programa)*, Projecto de Reabilitação Social Pós-Conflicto (PRSPC), Luanda, November 2002.

Ministério da Assistencia e Reinserção Social/Banco Mundial-IDA, *Operacionalização da Estratégia de Apoio a Reinserção Social* (volume 2, Documentos de Apoio), Projecto de Reabilitação Social Pós-Conflicto (PRSPC), Luanda, November 2002.

Ministério da Saúde. *Dados Demográficos da Província do Bié/2002*, Gabinete do Plano e Estatística, Departamento de Saude Publica, 2004.

N de Watteville, *Addressing gender issues in demobilisation and reintegration programmes*, Africa Region Working Paper Series, World Bank, 2002.

I Nübler, "Human resources development and utilization in demobilization and reintegration programs," *Bonn International Center for Conversion Paper 7*, January 1997.

Office for the Coordination of Humanitarian Affairs in Angola (OCHA). *Humanitarian Update*, 2002-2004.

United Nations, Consolidated Inter-Agency Appeal for Angola, Part I, November 2002.

Office for the Coordination of Humanitarian Affairs in Angola (OCHA), *Provincial Emergency Plans of Action for Resettlement and Return*, August 2002.

O Monteiro e A Caetano de Sousa. *Descentralização em Angola*, in *A Descentralização em Angola*, Programa das Nações Unidas para o Desenvolvimento (PNUD), March 2002.

I Parsons, *Beyond the Silencing of Guns: Demobilisation, Disarmament and Reintegration, Accord*, Issue 15, Conciliation Resources, 2004.

I Parsons, *Challenges of Reintegrating UNITA Ex-Combatants in Angola: Building a Post-conflict State*, Bonn International Centre for Conversion, available at <http://www.bicc.de/events/angola_conference/pdf/parsons.pdf>.

I Parsons, *Reconstructing Angola*, Global Insight, Institute for Global Dialogue, November 2003.

I Parsons, "Youth, Conflict & Identity: Political Mobilisation and Subjection in Angola," in *Mobilisation and Demobilisation: Youth and War in Africa*, Institute for Security Studies, Pretoria, 2005.

Praxis Group, *Background Paper Drafted as preparation for the ECHA Working Group Paper, "Harnessing Institutional Capacities in support of DDR of Former Combatants,"* Praxis Group Ltd, 6 June 2000.

Província da Huíla, Grupo Provincial de Análise da Vulnerabilidade. *Avaliação da Vulnerabilidade da População à Insegurança Alimentar Novembro/03 a Abril/04*, Lubango, May 2004.

Província do Bié, Grupo Provincial de Análise da Vulnerabilidade. *Avaliação da Vulnerabilidade da População à Insegurança Alimentar: Novembro 2003 a Abril 2004*, Kuíto, May 2004.

Província do Huambo, Grupo Provincial de Avaliação da Vulnerabilidade. *Avaliação da Vulnerabilidade da População à Insegurança Alimentar Novembro/03 a Abril/04*, Huambo, May 2004.

Republica de Angola. *Huambo: Perfil Socio-económico*, April 2003.

Republica de Angola. *Huila – Perfil Socio-económico*, Abril 2003.

Republica de Angola. *Perfil Provincial do Bié*, April 2003.

P Robson, "Communities and Reconstruction in Angola: The Prospects for Reconstruction in Angola from the Community Perspective," *Development Workshop Occasional Paper* 1, 2001.

United Nations, *Angola: the post-war challenges*, Common Country Assessment, 2002.

Universidade Católica de Angola, *Relatório Económico de Angola 2002*, Centro de Estudos e Investigação Científica, October 2003.

World Bank, *Aide Memoire: Angola demobilisation and reintegration program*, World Bank, Luanda, October 17, 2002.

World Bank, *Aide-Memoire: Angola Demobilisation and Reintegration Program*, Luanda, August 16, 2002.

World Bank, *Aide-Memoire: Angola Demobilisation and Reintegration Program*, Luanda, June 4, 2002.

World Bank, *Angola country report*, September 29- October, 2002.

World Food Programme, *Angola: Vulnerability Assessment in Rural Areas - National Overview*, Vulnerability Analysis and Food Aid Working Group Chaired by WFP/VAM Unit, Luanda, June 2004.

SURVEY QUESTIONNAIRE

Questionário Para Desmobilizados de Luena _____   Número: ☐

Data _____   Código geográfico _____

Entrevistador _____   Relator _____

1. Província _____   2. Município _____

3. Comuna _____   4. Ombala _____

5. Imbo linene _____   6. Imbo _____

I. Identificação

7. Nome do entrevistado _____

8. Idade ☐

9. Sexo   a. Masculino ☐   b. Feminino ☐

10. Origem   Província _____   Município _____

11. Estado Civil a. casado(a) ☐   b. união de facto ☐   c. divorciado(a) ☐
                  d. separado(a) ☐   e. solteiro(a) ☐   f. viúvo(a) ☐
                  g. Outro ☐ **indica** _____

12. Tem quaisquer outras relações conjugais?   a. Sim ☐   b. Não ☐
    Se sim, detalhes _____

13. Habilitações literárias a. I nível ☐   b. II nível ☐   c. III nível ☐
                             d. Médio ☐   e. Universitário ☐   f. analfabeto ☐

14. Religião   a. Protestante ☐   b. Católico ☐   c. Sem religião ☐
                 d. Outro ☐ _____

15. Língua materna a. Umbundu ☐   b. Kimbundu ☐   c. Nganguela ☐
                    d. Outro ☐ _____

16. Outras línguas faladas em casa a. Umbundu ☐   b. Kimbundu ☐   c. Nganguela ☐
                                    d. Tchokwe ☐   e. Kikongo ☐   f. Português ☐
                                    g. Outro ☐ _____

II. Desmobilização & Retorno

17. Chegou aqui há quantos meses atras? _____

18. Veio sozinho ou acompanhado?   a. Sozinho   ☐
                                    b. Acompanhado ☐ **por quem?** _____

19. Este é o seu local de nascimento?   a. Sim ☐ **[Salte para a pergunta 21]**
                                        b. Não ☐ **[Salte para a pergunta 20]**

20. Se não for seu local de nascimento: Já aqui viveu anteriormente?
   a. Sim, antes da vida militar   ☐
   b. Sim, durante a vida militar   ☐
   c. Não, nunca   ☐ **[Salte para a pergunta 22]**

21. Se nasceu aqui ou se viveu aqui antes: Quando partiu pela ultima vez?

_____

22. Tens família/familiares aqui? a. Sim ☐ **Quem?** _____
                                   b. Não ☐

23. Porquê escolheu de vir por aqui?
   a. Porque é terra natal / dos pais ☐ **Quem?** _____
   b. Para encontrar a família   ☐
   c. Acompanhando esposo/a   ☐
   d. Acompanhando amigo(s)   ☐
   e. Este lugar foi indicado   ☐ **Por quem?** _____
   f. Perspectivas económicas   ☐ **Quais?** _____
   g. Outro   ☐ **Indica** _____

24. O que fazia antes de ir ao serviço militar? (actividade principal)
   a. Biscatos   ☐ **Para quem?** _____
   b. Camponês   ☐
   c. Agricultor   ☐
   d. Empregado/a   ☐ **Indica** _____
   e. Negócio   ☐ **Tipo** _____
   f. Estudava   ☐ **Indica nível** _____
   g. Era criança   ☐
   h. Outro   ☐ **Indica** _____

25. Teve alguma formação profissional (antes de ir ao serviço militar)?
   a. Não, nenhuma   ☐
   b. Alfabetização ☐
   c. Mecânico   ☐
   d. Motorista   ☐
   e. Pedreiro   ☐
   f. Enfermeiro   ☐
   g. Professor   ☐
   h. Outro   ☐ **Indica** _____

26. Em que ano ingressou no serviço militar? _____

27. Qual foi o seu tempo de permanência no exército? ☐ anos   ☐ meses

28. Qual foi a sua patente no exército?
   a. Coronel ☐   b. Major ☐   c. Capitão ☐   d. Tenente ☐
   e. Alferes ☐   f. Aspirante ☐   g. Sargento ☐   h. 2º Sargento ☐
   i. Raso ☐   j. Outro ☐ _____

29. Recebeu alguma formação profissional durante o serviço militar?
   a. Não, nenhuma ☐
   b. Alfabetização ☐
   c. Acompanhando esposo/a ☐
   d. Motorista ☐
   e. Pedreiro ☐
   f. Enfermeiro ☐
   g. Professor ☐
   h. Outro ☐ **Indica** _____

30. Onde foi desmobilizado? **(centro de acolhimento)** _____

31. Tem os documentos de desmobilização? a. Sim, todos ☐
                                           b. Alguns mas não todos ☐
                                           c. Não, nenhum ☐

32. Recebeu o kit de desmobilização?   a. Sim ☐   b. Não ☐

33. Recebeu o subsidio de contingência? a. Sim ☐   b. Não ☐

34. Quais eram os seus principais desejos logo após a desmobilização?
   a. Continuar com os estudos ☐
   b. Formação profissional ☐ **qual?** _____
   c. Arranjar um emprego ☐ **qual?** _____
   d. Adquirir/construir casa ☐
   e. Adquirir terra para cultivar ☐
   f. Ir ao encontro da família ☐
   g. Assegurar a paz ☐
   h. Outro ☐ **indica** _____

35. Estes desejos estão sendo realizados? a. Sim ☐
                                           b. Não ☐ **Porquê?** _____

36. Já foi desmobilizado anteriormente? [durante Bicesse ou Lusaka]
   a. Sim ☐   **quando** [_____]   e onde [_____]
   b. Não ☐

III. Situação Sócio Económica Actual

37. O entrevistado é o chefe da família?   a. Sim ☐   b. Não ☐

38. Se não, o chefe da família é o seu/a sua
   a. Esposo/a ☐   b. Filho(a) ☐   c. Pai/Mãe ☐
   d. Irmão/irmã ☐   e. Primo(a) ☐   f. Tio/a) ☐
   g. Outro ☐ _____

39. A casa em que vive é de quem?
   a. Própria ☐   b. Da família/familiares ☐   c. Alugada ☐
   d. Emprestada ☐   e. Sem casa ☐

40. Tem acesso a terra arável para cultivar?   a. Sim ☐
                                    b. Não ☐ **[salte para a pergunta 43]**

41. Se sim, quantos dias de charrua cultivou este ano? ☐

42. Se sim, esta terra é: a. própria? ☐   b. alugada? ☐   c. emprestada? ☐

43. Quantos pessoas vivem na sua casa? _____

44. Quem são as pessoas que vivem na sua casa? (ex. quantos filhos, órfãos, outros...)
_____

45. Quantos contribuem para o sustento da família?
   a. Só o entrevistado ☐
   b. Duas pessoas (entrevistado e esposo/a) ☐
   c. Mais de duas pessoas ☐

46. Tem mais família próxima noutro local (ex. filhos/esposa)?
   a. Sim ☐ **Quem?** _____
   b. Não ☐ **[salte para a pergunta 48]**

47. Se sim espera que ele/s(a/s) se venham juntar a si no futuro?
   a. Sim ☐ **Quando?** _____
   b. Não ☐ **Porquê?** _____

48. Ocupação / actividade económica principal:
   a. Biscatos ☐ **Para quem?** _____
   b. Camponês ☐
   c. Agricultor ☐
   d. Empregado/a ☐ **Empregador** _____
   e. Negócio ☐ **Tipo** _____
   f. Estudava ☐ **Indica nível** _____
   g. Outro ☐ **Indica** _____

49. Tem outras fontes de rendimentos / alimentação?
   a. Biscatos   ☐ **Para quem?** _____
   b. Da família   ☐ **Quem?** _____
   c. Duma ONG/PAM   ☐ **Qual?** _____
   d. Da administração ☐ **O quê?** _____
   e. Outro   ☐ **Quem?** _____

50. Acha que tem direito ao emprego e à formação profissional? a. Sim ☐   b. Não ☐

51. Se sim, quem será responsável para fornecer esses? _____

52. Está integrado em algum projecto ligado aos ex-combatentes?
   a. Sim ☐ **Detalhes:** _____
   b. Não ☐

53. É membro de alguma organização/grupo? a. Sim ☐
                                            b. Não ☐ **[salte para a pergunta 56]**

54. **Se sim**, de que tipo?
   a. Religiosa   ☐   b. Política   ☐   c. Cívica   ☐
   d. Desportiva ☐   e. Tradicional ☐
   Qual / quais? _____

55. Se sim, ocupa algum cargo de responsabilidade nessa organização?
   a. Sim ☐ **Indica** _____
   b. Não ☐

55. Se sim, ocupa algum cargo de responsabilidade nessa organização?
   a. Sim ☐ **Indica** _____
   b. Não ☐

56. É membro duma igreja?
   a. Sim ☐ **Qual?** _____
   b. Não ☐ **[salte para a pergunta 58]**

57. Se sim, esta igreja tem presença aqui? a. Sim ☐   b. Não ☐

58. Foi membro duma igreja antes da vida militar?
   a. Sim ☐
   b. Sim, mas uma outra igreja/denominação ☐
   c. Não, nenhuma ☐

59. Foi membro duma igreja durante a vida militar?
   a. Sim ☐
   b. Sim, mas uma outra igreja/denominação ☐
   c. Não, nenhuma ☐

60. Com quem passa mais o seu tempo ? (pode escolher mais do quem um)
    a. Minha família ☐
    b. Membros/amigos da minha igreja ☐
    c. Membros de outro grupo / organização ☐
    d. Outros ex-combatentes ☐
    e. Outros **(identifica quem)** ☐

61. A quem recorre mais vezes quando tem dificuldades?
    a. Igreja ☐   b. Soba ☐   c. Esposo/a ☐
    d. Família ☐   e. Administrador ☐   f. Partido ☐
    g. Outro ☐ _____

62. Quando estava na vida militar, a quem recorrias quando tinha dificuldades?
    a. Igreja ☐   b. Soba ☐   c. Esposo/a ☐
    d. Família ☐   e. Administrador ☐   f. Partido ☐
    g. Outro ☐ _____

63. Quem considera como pessoa mais importante na comunidade?
    a. Pastor/catequista ☐   b. Soba ☐   c. Administrador ☐
    d. Outro ☐ _____

IV. Reintegração

64. Neste momento, considera-se
    a. Civil ☐   b. Militar ☐   c. Desmobilizado ☐

65. Considera-se reintegrado na vida civil?   a. Sim ☐   b. Não ☐

66. Se não, o que é que poderia facilitar a sua reintegração na vida civil?
    a. Formação profissional ☐
    b. Emprego ☐
    c. Terra para cultivar ☐
    d. Outro comportamento da comunidade ☐
    e. Outro ☐ **Indica** _____

67. Alguma vez pensou regressar a vida militar?   a. Sim ☐   b. Não ☐
    Se sim porquê?

68. Neste momento, quais são os seus principais desejos(planos) em relação ao futuro?

a. Continuar com os estudos ☐
b. Formação profissional ☐
c. Arranjar um emprego ☐ **qual?** _____
d. Adquirir/construir casa ☐
e. Adquirir terra para cultivar ☐
f. Ir ao encontro da família ☐
g. Assegurar a paz ☐
h. Outro ☐ **Indica** _____

69. Pensa que foi bem recebido pela comunidade?

a. Sim ☐
b. Não ☐ **Porquê?** _____

70. O que fizeram para te receber? [Pode ser mais do que um]

a. Arranjaram terra / casa para nós ☐
b. Deram-nos comida ☐
c. Deram-nos outras coisas ☐ **quais?** _____
d. Fizeram uma reunião ☐
e. Fizeram uma cerimónia ☐ **descreve** _____
f. Outro ☐ **indica** _____

71. Espera ficar aqui?

a. Sim ☐ **[salte para pergunta 73]**
b. Não ☐

72. Porque pensa sair?

a. É difícil ganhar a vida aqui ☐
b. Não se sente a vontade com a comunidade aqui ☐
c. Tem problemas com indivíduos específicos ☐
d. As possibilidades são melhores em outros sítios ☐
e. Outras razões **(indica)** _____

73. Se houver uma possibilidade de transferir para uma outra área, preferia ficar ou transferir?

a. Ficar ☐   b. Transferir ☐

74. Porquê? _____
_____

75. Como pensa que os desmobilizados poderão contribuir para assegurar a paz no país?

a. Não têm este poder ☐
b. Com o seu trabalho ☐
c. Por meio do perdão / reconciliação ☐
d. Outro ☐ **Indica** _____

76. Já ouviu falar das próximas eleições?
   a. Sim ☐
   b. Não ☐ **[salte para a pergunta 76]**

77. Se sim, quem falou?
   a. Representante do Governo ☐
   b. Representante do MPLA ☐
   c. Representante da UNITA ☐
   d. Representante de um outro partido ☐
   e. ONG ☐
   f. Rádio ☐
   g. O soba ☐
   h. Pessoas da comunidade ☐
   i. Outros ☐ **Quem?** _____

78. Já tens conhecimento de alguns partidos políticos?
   a. Sim ☐ **Quais** _____
   b. Não ☐

79. Na sua opinião votar é:
   a. Uma obrigação decidida pelo Governo/Administração ☐
   b. Uma obrigação decidida pela UNITA ☐
   c. Um direito que lhe é dado por ser Angolano que posso ou não usar ☐
Se outra resposta, indica

80. Acha que as eleições são importantes para a consolidação da paz?
   a. Sim ☐
   b. Não ☐
Se sim, como?

81. Votou nas eleições de 1992?
   a. Sim ☐
   b. Não ☐